LIVES OF JESUS

GOD, JEW, REBEL, THE HIDDEN JESUS

AN INVESTIGATION INTO THE

LIVES OF JESUS

MARK TULLY

BBC BOOKS

This book is published to accompany
the television series *Lives of Jesus*,
first broadcast in 1996
Producer: Angela Tilby

Designed by Tim Higgins
Maps by Venture Graphics
Picture research by Deirdre O'Day

ISBN 0 563 37148 X

First published in 1996 by BBC Books,
an imprint of BBC Worldwide Publishing.
BBC Worldwide Limited,
Woodlands, 80 Wood Lane, London W12 0TT

Set in Sabon and Berkeley Oldstyle Medium
by Ace Filmsetting Ltd, Frome, Somerset
Printed and bound in Great Britain by
Butler & Tanner Limited, Frome and London
Colour separations by
Radstock Repro Limited, Midsomer Norton
Jacket printed by
Lawrence Allen Limited, Weston-super-Mare

Contents

Introduction

Whenever I told anyone I was presenting a television series and writing a book called *Lives of Jesus* I was asked two questions – why *Lives*, plural, and why you?

The *Lives* plural is because there has been an explosion of scholarly interest over the last twenty-five years in discovering more about Jesus the man – who he was, what he believed, what he taught, and, perhaps most important of all, how he perceived his relationship to God. Some fascinating new material has been uncovered for scholars to consider. The discovery and translation of the Dead Sea Scrolls has revealed new knowledge about the different sects of the Jewish world, which was the world of Jesus. The discovery of the Gospel of St Thomas, which was not in the New Testament, has revealed new sayings attributed to Jesus. Archaeologists have continued their investigations, producing sometimes divergent conclusions about life in first-century Palestine and the religion of first-century Jews. The study of theology in universities has also broadened and it is no longer a near-monopoly of the Churches. All the scholars studying the history of Jesus whom I have met, whether clerics or not, have insisted that they are historians, uninfluenced by faith, as rigorous in their scholarship as those who study any other figure of the past. They are now bringing knowledge gained in other fields to bear on their subject: fresh insights have been acquired from comparative religion, sociology, anthropology, economics and, of course, archaeology. The result of all this scholarly activity has been to produce different schools of interpretation, with their advocates arguing fiercely that they alone hold the key to understanding Jesus. They are the *Lives of Jesus*.

And why me? That's perhaps a harder question to answer. I am certainly not a scholar. I am a journalist, a profession not always regarded very kindly by scholars. But journalists do have a role as simplifiers of scholarship. When professional historians write they always have the spectre of other scholars standing over them. They have to cover their backs to make sure that they have left no room for their rivals to pour scorn on them. That inevitably means that they tend to write in greater detail than the general reader can take on board, although I hasten to add I have read some very readable books by scholars of Jesus. At the same time historians have their own axe to grind, and so they are not necessarily the best people to report on the whole field of scholarship. But I have always believed that the best journalism is written by those who have an interest in their subject. I would go further, and say they should be in sympathy with it. It is, I believe, a mistake to think that journalists must be hostile. From my youngest days I have been fascinated by Jesus, and although I could not claim to be a card-carrying Christian I am certainly no sceptic.

But I do not want to give the impression that this is my book alone. I owe a debt to all scholars I have interviewed, who gave generously of their time and kindly allowed me to quote them. This book is based on the work of the BBC North production team responsible for the television series *Lives of Jesus*: Chris Salt, Rosemary Dawson, Anna Cox, Moira Kean and Ros Nevin. I owe them all a profound debt. I am particularly indebted to Angela Tilby, the series producer, who has acted as my theological censor, reading every word of this book and making many suggestions and alterations. Without her support I would never have had the courage to write the book, but at the same time I have to take the final responsibility for what you are about to read.

There is one last question that readers might ask: why now? The answer is easy. The year of publication, 1996, is the most widely accepted date for the two thousandth anniversary of the birth of Jesus. We are also approaching the millennium. So surely this is the right time to look again at the man whose influence has been so profound that we still date the start of the first millennium from the year in which tradition says he was born.

1

Jesus the God

A Two-thousand-year-old Tradition

It is not very fashionable nowadays to support compulsory worship, but as a young child I enjoyed starting the morning singing hymns. At my first boarding school in the town of Darjeeling, high in the Himalayas and rightly famed for its unique tea, I can still remember which hymn was my favourite: 'Immortal, invisible, God only wise'. After the war I went on to a prep school in Britain, where I never objected to daily chapel. At my public school, Marlborough, I developed such a taste for it that I attended almost every voluntary service as well as the daily compulsory worship. Recently I went back to give a lecture at Marlborough and found to my dismay that my appearance was an *alternative* to chapel. Even a school founded for the sons of the Anglican clergy – which I am not, incidentally – apparently no longer insisted that all the pupils should go to chapel on Sundays.

I was not particularly pious at school, and I was not particularly well behaved either, but chapel made such a deep impact on me that I read theology at university, and even went on to prepare for ordination. But after two terms at theological college I was told that I belonged more in the public house than the pulpit. My regular attendance at the Adam and Eve, on the hill leading up to Lincoln Cathedral, made this judgement difficult to argue against. I have certainly not led an orthodox Christian life since then, but I have retained my love of Anglican worship and my fascination with the figure

The west front of Wells Cathedral showing Christ in Majesty
seated between the cherubim, his right hand raised
in blessing. Beneath him are the Apostles.

of Jesus. If I'm honest I would say that I still share the hope of the Church, if not the faith. I would like to believe that one day I might even recover that faith. So I stand in the long line, stretching back two thousand years, of those whose lives have been profoundly influenced by Jesus.

As we approach the millennium, the influence of the Churches is in such decline that it is no longer felt necessary to ensure that children are given the opportunity I was given of learning what a theologian recently described to me as 'the language of Christianity'. So this is surely an appropriate time to consider whether the line I stand in will come to an end, whether the belief in Jesus as God which has underpinned Christianity will survive the next thousand years.

But though the Churches are not doing very well, at least in Britain, it is my experience that there is still a great interest in religion. Living in India, I am struck by the number of people who come from Britain and other parts of Europe to see whether Hinduism or Buddhism will fill the vacuum they feel in their lives. Why are they not satisfied with Christianity? I am given many explanations, but the one I hear most often is that Christianity no longer makes any sense.

Eastern religions do not require commitment to any particular creed – just a mind open to the existence of the divine. The problem with Christianity is that it demands belief in one specific person, who performed miracles and was miraculously raised from the dead. That person is, of course, Jesus. In one sense, Jesus is not a problem. There is no difficulty in believing that a remarkable man existed in first-century Palestine; there is plenty of historical evidence for that, from those who followed him and those who did not. What is much harder to believe is that Jesus was divine, and that in his death on the cross he offered a unique sacrifice to redeem us. As the hymn says, 'Once, only once, and once for all his precious life he gave'. Why should God, who is immortal, choose a particular moment to intervene in history? Why did God elect a particular people to witness this unique demonstration of his love for humanity? If belief in the redeeming power of Jesus is the only way to salvation, does God exclude all those who have never had the chance to hear the Christian message? Christianity is so particular and specific that to many people it is incredible.

The historical Jesus: opposing viewpoints

The credibility of Christianity has not been helped by arguments among historians and theologians about the details of the Gospel stories. These are pounced on by journalists who are not particularly prone to publishing stories which favour the claims of Christianity. A recent example was a row which blew up when a group of American scholars brought out the results of a series of seminars. They had met over a number of years with the intention of establishing what Jesus really said. The scholars considered all the evidence from the Bible, and added to it reported sayings from other early Christian writings. They worked through it all, verse by verse, using a method of voting which reminds me of the old-fashioned black-balling of undesirable members of clubs. Scholars who regarded a saying of Jesus as definitely authentic dropped a red bead into a bucket, a pink bead signified likelihood but not certainty, a blue bead that the saying was probably in harmony with the teaching of Jesus but was not uttered by him, and a black bead meant that the saying was certainly inauthentic. Their version of the Gospels, printed in the four colours, made their conclusions startlingly clear. So much of the Gospel story has been black-beaded that only 18 per cent of the sayings of Jesus are even in the pink category. There is not a single red-beaded saying in the whole of St John's Gospel. The scholars took the view that less than a quarter of the sayings attributed to Jesus in the New Testament Gospels were really said by him.

The results of the Jesus Seminar, as it is called, have been challenged by many reputable scholars. Some have argued that the criteria used to judge the Gospels are not valid, and that evidence which supports a far greater element of historical accuracy has been ignored. Others have described the whole enterprise as futile and have returned to the position of the great German scholar Rudolf Bultmann who, back in the 1920s, advised against searching for the historical Jesus, warning, 'We can know almost nothing concerning the life and personality of Jesus'. Bultmann believed the Gospels to be so far removed from the original Jesus that they could not tell us much about him. The figure of Jesus in the Gospels reflected the struggles and preoccupations of the early Church, and it was the early Church which put the stories and sayings about Jesus into the four Gospel narratives that we have today. Bultmann did not think we could get any further back than that, and he advised Christian scholars to concentrate on the Christ of faith, the Christ preached by the Church.

But for most Christians that is not good enough. The Jesus of history really matters, simply because the claims of Christianity are rooted in history. It is a sobering fact that the only Churches which are expanding in Britain are those of the extreme Protestants, who often take a literal view of the Bible and claim that every word of Jesus reported in the Gospels must have been said by him. They stand in the opposite corner to the Jesus Seminar, many even believing in a six-day creation. The growth of literalism is perhaps not surprising for many Christians feel their faith is under threat from the materialism and cynicism of our times. When devout people feel their religion is threatened they often take refuge in what is now known as fundamentalism, shutting their ears to all critical interpretation. The same literalism can be observed in modern Islam: many Muslims believe their religion is under threat from Western materialism.

As I see it, those Protestants demand too much certainty and end up with an unreal Jesus, insulated from legitimate historical inquiry. But does that mean we have to leave Jesus in the hands of those who believe little or nothing of what the Gospels say? Some sceptical scholars are devout Christians and claim that their way is the safest because they are constructing a new, non-miraculous Jesus in whom we can believe, whose life can be reconciled with the expectations of historians and scientists. But their rationalized Jesus is not the only one on offer. There are other scholars who maintain that, even after applying the most rigid standards of scholarship, the great tradition of Jesus as the unique Son of God remains intact.

The cathedrals of England are monuments to the survival of faith in Jesus the divine. Whether it be Durham or Lincoln, on hilltops dominating their cities; Ely, a landmark in the flat fens; Canterbury, York, Winchester or Wells; the great cathedrals have survived the upheavals of the Reformation, the Civil War and the Industrial Revolution, and are still places where the divine Jesus is worshipped every day. If you compare them with the castles

The fourteenth-century chancel arch of Wells Cathedral.
The 'scissors' design is unique to Wells. Many cathedrals and churches
have a 'rood' – an elevated crucifix with the Virgin Mary and St John – on
a beam or screen separating the nave from the chancel.

which were built at the same time, you see how durable the monuments to faith have proved over the monuments of secular power. The castles that do survive as anything more than ruins are museums; reminders of the past, not part of life today. The rulers who built the castles have come and gone; their way of life has long since disappeared. Faith in Jesus lives on to this day.

Wells proudly boasts that it is the smallest cathedral city in England. I went there to meet two of the scholars who believe that the American Jesus Seminar has got it wrong, and that the Jesus of the Gospels has not been disproved by history. As I crossed the green lawn of the cathedral close I looked up to see the dramatic west front, with its statues flanking the central window and spreading across the two towers. There were secular rulers, kings and their knights. There were men of God, the Apostles and other saints. There were supernatural beings: cherubim, seraphim and angels of the Resurrection. Standing at the pinnacle of the west front, ruling over them all, was the figure of Christ in Majesty.

Just outside the door which visitors use there was a notice requesting – not, I am glad to say, demanding – contributions for the maintenance of the cathedral. I passed through the door and entered the nave. There my eye was drawn immediately to the most unusual arch at the end of the aisle. It is really two arches. One is inverted, standing on the tip of the other, giving the impression of scissors. In the upturned arch stood a crucifix. Jesus on the cross looked down on the pews where the congregation would sit. Below the lower arch was an altar where the sacrifice that Jesus made was celebrated in the Eucharist. The west front and the scissors arch brought together in this cathedral the two cardinal beliefs of Christianity: that Jesus was divine, but that he was also a man who felt all the humiliation and pain of a brutal execution.

The first scholar I met was Tom Wright, an Anglican priest and the Dean of Lichfied Cathedral. He had earlier taught the New Testament at Oxford and Cambridge and at McGill University in Canada. Walking up a staircase, its stone well worn by the clergy who for nearly seven centuries have climbed them to get to the chapter house, Tom Wright told me he had known he was destined to be ordained in the Anglican Church from the age of eight. This was following in the footsteps of his mother's family, which had produced a number of clergymen; although there had been moments of confusion when he had wondered why he wasn't going into his father's family timber business. Tom Wright was wearing a polo-neck sweater and tweed jacket, not his clerical collar.

We entered the chapter house with the sunlight streaming through the long windows, and sat on the base of the pillar supporting the high vaulted roof. Before we started the interview Tom Wright combed the fringe of hair round his bald head, saying, 'I don't want to look like a mad professor.' Perhaps that wasn't entirely necessary. He actually looked quite conventional, with his short, well-cut hair and his neat, black beard streaked with grey.

Tom Wright has never ducked historical issues. He has always insisted that Jesus must be studied as a historical figure because the claims of Christianity are historical. But I suggested that being a priest might bias his interpretation of history. He replied, 'Yes there is a problem in people's minds because many of those who are doing this historical work on Jesus are themselves committed Christians. But then there are also many scholars who come from other backgrounds like agnosticism, or the Jewish faith. The key thing to grasp is that nobody is neutral – you can't just be a fly on the wall in this debate. Some people may hope to find a Jesus to base their faith on, others go looking for a Jesus to base their agnosticism on. The critical question could be put like this. Would you rather hear a lecture on Bach or Beethoven by somebody who was tone deaf, or by somebody who had given their life to performing, practising and engaging with the music?'

Tom had recently written a book refuting some of the more outlandish theories about the life of Jesus which had been published in the early 1990s. These included the widely publicized hypothesis that Jesus married Mary Magdalene, had children by her, then divorced her and remarried. His book would not have carried so much weight if he had not been able to produce sober historical evidence to counter such sensational claims.

The origins of Jesus's divinity

So how much do we really know about Jesus? Tom assured me that there is independent evidence, unconnected with the Gospels or Christianity, to show that Jesus existed. Two Roman historians, Tacitus and Pliny, write about him; as does the Jewish historian Josephus. All agree that he lived in Palestine at the time of the Roman Emperor Augustus. But there has been so much confusion about the history of Jesus that there are people who even doubt that fact, who think the Church made it all up. Most of our knowledge of Jesus comes from the New Testament: from the four Gospels and from the letters of Paul and other early Christians which came to be regarded as sacred scripture. Tom Wright told me that the New Testament shows that belief in the divinity of Jesus arrived very early. It was not, as some have suggested, a later invention of the Church. He said, 'Our earliest written evidence is St Paul, and he refers to and quotes from things which may well predate him. In other words we are going back to the first twenty years or so of Christianity. There are passages in Paul where, almost as a throwaway remark, he puts Jesus and God together, for instance, "Blessed be the God and Father of Our Lord Jesus Christ. Grace to you and peace from God the Father and the Lord Jesus Christ." '

Tom then went on to quote from St Paul's First Epistle to the Corinthians, 'For us there is one God and Father from whom are all things, and for whom we exist, and one Lord Jesus Christ, through whom are all things, and through whom we exist.' He explained to me that this is an adapted version of the *shema*, the central Jewish prayer which devout Jews say every day. In its usual form it begins, 'Hear, O Israel, the Lord your God, the Lord is one.' That prayer is a statement of the fundamental article of the Jewish faith, that there is only one God. Yet here is Paul, himself a Jew, combining Jesus with that one God. As Tom put it, 'St Paul was saying, "I am a God-*and*-Jesus monotheist".'

So within twenty years of Jesus dying we know there were leading Christians who believed that he was divine. But it still didn't answer the question, 'Where did St Paul get this idea from?'

To provide an answer, Tom reminded me that Jews learnt from the Hebrew scriptures – our Old Testament – of a God who was 'passionate and compassionate and whose heart bled for his people'. He had already shown his power and care at the beginning of their history as a nation by leading them out of slavery in Egypt. He had ruled them through judges and through chosen kings, and when they had fallen on hard times he had promised that he would rescue them. At the time of Jesus the Jews were expecting some divine intervention. He went on to explain how Jesus had come to be interpreted as God's long-expected act of mercy: 'I think the whole life, message and teaching of Jesus makes its own powerful Messianic statement.' Tom reminded me that in the Old Testament God alone can forgive sinners.

He thought that by offering forgiveness to sinners, Jesus was making a claim that he had the power to exercise God's prerogative. Usually forgiveness was only available through sacrifices in the Temple in Jerusalem. Jesus was highly critical of the Temple and its sacrificial system. I asked Tom whether the fact that Jesus rode into Jerusalem on a donkey, and spoke powerfully against the Temple, would have been seen as a claim to be God's Messiah, the successor to King David.

Tom replied, 'Yes. That's a very Messianic thing to do. It says Jesus is the real king. He is the one sent by God to be our rescuer, our saviour, our deliverer.'

'But he didn't die like a king, he died like a criminal,' I countered.

Tom said, 'You're right. Messiahs don't die on crosses. Messiahs defeat the occupying forces. The whole game would have been over right there if it hadn't been for the Resurrection. Nothing would have got off the ground. In terms of first-century Jewish history it seems to be very clear that nothing would have happened next.'

That Christianity did get off the ground is a fact of history, and certainly one possible explanation for it is that the Resurrection actually happened. Many other historians less committed to Christianity than Tom accept that a very powerful event must have taken place after Jesus died which radically changed his followers. Tom went on to explain that, in his view, it was the Resurrection which persuaded the early Christians that Jesus was divine. 'It was because Jesus rose from the dead that his followers were forced to reflect on the fuller, deeper meaning of his prophetic and Messianic life. They also had to make some sense of his death. I think they realized that what he had accomplished in that whole total package was precisely what the Bible says God is going to do for his people. He has returned to them. He has saved them and set them free.'

After talking to Tom, whose ideas seemed sensible and scholarly, I found myself reflecting on why there is so much scepticism about the Gospel stories. I think the problem is that Christians have often spoken, and indeed still do speak, of the Bible as 'The Word of God'. To those who are not scholars, that phrase implies that the Gospel stories must always be the literal truth. When it is made clear that this cannot be so, not least because there are four different accounts, many reject them altogether. If someone casts doubt on just one event in Jesus's life, such as the Virgin Birth, he is assumed to be saying that all the Church's claims are untrue. But as a journalist I have learnt that there is no such thing as absolute truth in reporting what has happened. Journalists can and should report facts accurately. Their reports should certainly not contain lies. Even that is not always easy, especially when reporting events which happened some time ago. Memory is unreliable at a distance. Then there is the problem of selection, or editing. Which of the many facts available are you to report, in what order, and to leave what impression? Later, historians of our times will use newspapers as one of their sources, but they will need to interpret the reports in the light of the politics of each paper. They will need to take account of the readers that each paper aimed to attract, and the advertising interests. When we look at the four Gospels we should not be surprised to see four rather different versions of the life of Jesus. Each one has been written from a particular viewpoint for a particular readership. That, of course, no more means that they consist of lies than do the differing reports in different newspapers.

The newspaper analogy can be taken too far. But it does at least show that we should expect the four Gospels to produce significantly different portraits of Jesus, without falling into the trap of thinking that the Gospels are therefore untrue. Of course, what we all tend to do is to blur bits of all four into an amalgam, with the result that we lose the distinctive flavour of each. Curiously, the early Church refused to do that, though you might think it would have been easier and more convenient to have one authorized Gospel than four different ones. Yet it says something about the Church's integrity that it left the four Gospels as they were without trying to blend them or tidy up their differences. That still leaves the question, what exactly are the Gospels? Are they a unique kind of writing, or can they be compared with other historical books?

Four Gospels, four interpretations

The Christian scholar Richard Burridge, the Dean of King's College, London, has conducted painstaking research into the Gospels, dividing their contents into different categories, counting verbs, subjects and objects, and comparing them to other literature of their time. He has concluded that we can at least understand the limits which history sets on our interpretation of Jesus, and those limits do allow for an early belief in his divinity.

To illustrate his point Richard Burridge took me to the library above the east cloister of Wells Cathedral. Built in the fifteenth century, it is a long corridor with a wooden roof and plain glass windows set just above the desks to give plenty of light. Some of the leather-bound books are still chained to the seventeenth-century shelves. Burridge, a ruddy-faced West Countryman, who without his clerical collar and the cross hanging round his neck might be taken for a farmer, removed a volume from the shelves. It was the Roman historian Tacitus's biography of his father-in-law Agricola, one of a number of priceless editions of ancient biographies kept at Wells. Burridge explained that his research had convinced him that the Gospels were composed in the genre of ancient biographies, and so in order to understand them scholars needed to compare the accounts of the life of Jesus with other biographies of their time.

He turned to Tacitus and said, 'The ancients were much more interested than we are in the symbolic or psychological meaning of a person's life.' I remembered from my classics classes that Tacitus gave no physical description of his main subject, Agricola, nor did he describe the events of his life as a modern biographer would. He just concentrated on a description of one crucial battle between the Roman soldiers whom Agricola commanded and an army of Scottish tribes. The reason he did so was because this battle, he believed, revealed all that was important about Agricola's nature. He included a long and moving speech by the Scottish chieftain which summed up exactly the moral dilemma at the heart not only of Agricola's life, but of Roman imperialism. The speech climaxed in the powerful phrase, 'The Romans create a wilderness and call it peace.' Richard Burridge explained to me, 'What Tacitus is saying through this statement is that this is the truth, this is what's happening here. The message of Agricola's life is that Roman Imperialism – and you have to remember that Tacitus was a Roman senator – brings slavery, and that's what we Romans need to face.'

'How does this relate to the Gospels?' I asked.

'We have to look at the Gospels with a first-century understanding of the notion of truth and the way in which facts relate to the truth, rather than understand them in terms of the twentieth-century debate between legend and facts.' Richard went on to explain to me that the Gospels, like Tacitus, are selective. They concentrate on the three years or so of Jesus's active ministry, a relatively short period. They all contain a lot of detail about the

last week of his life because the writers want us to interpret him in the light of the events which led to his death. 'Actually facts will never tell you anything true in one sense – you always have to interpret them.'

Richard said that the authors of each of the Gospels interpreted the facts of Jesus's life differently. They saw Jesus in different ways and were writing for different audiences. From early times the four Gospels were depicted by four symbolic beasts, who would have been familiar to the early Christians because they appeared as part of God's retinue in a vision of the prophet Ezekiel. The four beasts, or 'living creatures' as Ezekiel puts it, have the faces of a lion, a man, an ox and an eagle. St Mark's Gospel is represented as a lion. This is appropriate, because his Gospel is brief and to the point. Everything seems to happen at once. One of Mark's favourite words is 'immediately'. Mark's Jesus is a man of action rather than a teacher. There are only four parables in the whole Gospel. Jesus rushes to complete his task, to die as the Old Testament prophesied that the Messiah would. At the Crucifixion Jesus feels that God has deserted him. The curtain of the Temple is torn in two. Three women who go to the empty tomb are afraid of the young man they see, not understanding what has happened. St Mark's Gospel, like a lion, is frightening and direct, charging at high speed to reach its climax.

St Matthew's Gospel is portrayed as a human face. Matthew wanted to convince Jewish Christians that Jesus was the fulfilment of the Old Testament. His Jesus is a teacher, explaining what was said in Mark's Gospel and linking it to the promises that the Jews believed God had made. In Matthew's version of the Crucifixion Jesus makes clear that his role is to fulfil the Old Testament prophecy that the Messiah must die. But at the same time Matthew wanted Jewish Christians to agree that Gentiles could be accepted by the Church without fulfilling all the conditions of the Jewish law, and so he was very hard on the Jewish leaders of Jesus's time. St Matthew also goes out of

The four living creatures, symbols of the Four Evangelists:
the Man of St Matthew, the Lion of St Mark, the Ox of
St Luke and the Eagle of St John. The living creatures are
first described in the Old Testament Book of Ezekiel,
where they surround the wheels of God's chariot, and enter
Christian imagery with the visions of St John in the Book
of Revelation. From the Book of Kells, *c.* A D 800.

his way to insist that it was the Jewish leaders, not the Romans, who were responsible for Jesus's death – that Pilate was innocent.

The third Gospel, St Luke's, is portrayed as an ox. His Jesus bears our burdens for us, and is on the side of the poor and the oppressed. Even at the Crucifixion he is concerned for others. He prays for the women of Jerusalem and for the soldiers who nail him to the cross. He promises paradise to the penitent thief who hangs beside him. The ox was the universal beast of burden, and St Luke's Gospel was written for a universal audience.

The last Gospel, St John's, is represented as an eagle. The other three Gospels include much material in common, but St John's is quite different. Where the first three Gospels reveal who Jesus is by fleeting encounters, healings, arguments and parables, John is explicit. Jesus is the divine Son of God. He is the light and the life of the world. He is the word who has been with God from the beginning and is indeed God – hence the eagle soaring high above the world. Just before he dies on the cross Jesus says, 'It is finished.' God's purpose has been accomplished. In the other three Gospels Jesus is comparatively passive during the Passion story. In St John he remains in control, knowing what he has to do and carrying it through to the end. He is the word and wisdom of God in human form, 'The way, the truth and the life.'

Richard Burridge believes that St John's clear statement of the divinity of Jesus is implied, though less directly, in the other three Gospels. 'In Matthew, Mark, and Luke, Jesus makes a claim to be the *way* in that he receives and forgives sinners and brings them into the Kingdom of Heaven. So he is the way to God. He makes an implicit claim to be the *truth* through his teaching, his parables and all of that. He makes an implicit claim to be the *life* by healing and restoring people, or even raising them from the dead.' Richard Burridge thinks it unlikely that the very explicit statements that Jesus makes about his divinity in John's Gospel were all actually made by the historical Jesus. But by putting the words on Jesus's lips, John was witnessing to 'A truer Truth than facts can ever give.'

The four different interpretations of Jesus do not mean that the Gospel writers were telling different stories. Although they felt free to interpret the events in their own way, they told essentially the same story. Richard told me what might be called a parable to show how we are still left with one Jesus, not four. He said, 'It's like a ball park. The pitch has boundaries, and if you want to play the game you have to stay within the boundaries. The pictures of Jesus set out in the Gospels are the boundaries to what we can know about him. Running around on the field is the historical Jesus whom we can research. We can know quite a lot about him within the boundaries, but we can't tie him down because his position on the pitch is always moving. Yet there are boundaries, there are limits. You can't just create Jesus in any way you want.'

These two British scholars convinced me a historical case could be made for the Christian claim that Jesus was divine, a unique and once-for-all incarnation of God. Wells Cathedral, with what Tim Wright described as 'its walls soaked in prayer', reminded me of the power of that claim. But the claim cannot just be examined in a Christian context, by Christian scholars. These days it has to be examined more widely. Christianity is not the only religion, and its claims to uniqueness are under scrutiny now as never before.

Christianity in India

India is certainly not a Christian context: it is a predominantly Hindu country, with a large Muslim population too. Christians are in a tiny minority – under 3 per cent of the population. India is a place which does not seem very receptive to Jesus. The Christian missionaries, although backed by the might of Western imperialism, failed to make the sort of progress that they achieved in Africa or South America. The main Churches in India are now reluctant to make conversions for fear of offending Hindu or Muslim sentiments, and concentrate their energies on maintaining the toehold that the missionaries gained. But for all that, India is a good testing ground to discover whether the Christian claim that Jesus is divine really stands up: there are plenty of other gods to compare him with. It is also a good country in which to examine the Christian idea that there is only one way to salvation. India has offered a home to almost all the world's great religions, and has itself given birth to religions which, at first sight, seem to be almost the antithesis of Christianity because they teach that there are many ways to God.

Tradition has it that the Apostle Thomas first brought Christianity to India. He is often known as doubting Thomas, because he doubted the Resurrection. In Madras I visited the Little Mount, a shrine which has been built over the cave where St Thomas is believed to have lived. There I met a Roman

Catholic priest who proudly claimed that he was a Thomas Christian, and that the survival of his community was evidence that the Apostle had indeed come to India and converted people in the south to Christianity. He told me that the Apostle's mission to India was recorded in a third-century book called *The Acts of Thomas*. There is indeed good historical evidence for a Church existing in southern India from the fourth century.

When the Portuguese first came to India in the sixteenth century they found Christian communities with a long history, but the expansion of Christianity really started with their missionary efforts. One of the greatest European missionaries to India was Francis Xavier, who landed in the Portuguese colony of Goa in 1542 and brought papal rule to the region. His body is enshrined in the church of the Good Jesus at Goa. Although he made many converts, the subsequent history of Indian Christianity shows that it did not do much to change the lives of even those who did accept the missionaries' claim that Jesus was the only saviour.

The British came to India with the conviction that their culture was superior and that it was their duty to introduce it to those whom they thought had less civilized values. One of the greatest of the earlier British administrators in India, Sir Thomas Munro, wrote, 'Our sovereignty should be prolonged to the remotest possible period. . . . Whenever we are obliged to resign it, we should leave the natives so far improved from their connection with us, as to be capable of maintaining a free, or at least a regular, government amongst themselves.' We brought Christianity with us as part of what we thought was our 'civilizing mission'.

The British vision of the superiority of Western Christianity is enshrined in Calcutta Cathedral, appropriately dedicated to the greatest of all Christian missionaries, St Paul. The cathedral dominates the south-eastern corner of the Maidan, the Hyde Park of the city. Calcutta was once the capital of British India and the second city of the Empire. From the outside St Paul's looks like

St Francis Xavier (1506–52), dressed as a priest in a white stole, pouring baptismal water from a scallop shell over his kneeling converts. Xavier, a Jesuit, was one of the greatest Christian missionaries, whose journeys to save the heathen took him to India, Ceylon and Japan. Detail of a painting by Luca Giordano, seventeenth century.

a very English cathedral, built in the Gothic style. It even has a tower modelled on the Bell Harry tower of Canterbury Cathedral, the mother church of Anglicanism. It is set in a spacious close. When I attended Holy Communion there was a congregation of some two hundred and fifty people, almost all Indians. The pages of a version of the Anglican Prayer Book, in English, rustled in the breeze created by the fans wobbling precariously above the heads of the congregation. The Reverend Noel Sen, the vicar of the cathedral, was Indian too, but he read the service in an immaculate English accent. The hymns were also English. One was 'The Church's one foundation' with the rousing line at the end of each verse, 'One Church, one faith, one Lord'. I could not help reflecting that the Church, the faith and the Lord were English. I noticed that the Bengali service which followed was held in a side chapel and attended by only a handful of people. I was reminded of the notice board outside the church where I had made my Easter Communion the Sunday before, which announced very firmly, 'Services only in English.'

From the start, Calcutta Cathedral made few Concessions to India. It was built in the last century, a fitting memorial to one of the great missionaries, Bishop Reginald Heber, who became Bishop of Calcutta in 1823 and whose diocese stretched from India to Australia. His larger-than-life white marble statue still dominates the entrance to the cathedral. Bishop Heber was an outstanding Christian of his day. As an evangelical, he believed very firmly that salvation could only be achieved through a personal commitment to Jesus as the Son of God and an acceptance of the forgiveness he won for us by his sacrificial death on the cross. He wrote several well-known hymns including 'Holy, holy, holy, Lord God Almighty' and 'Brightest and best of the sons of the morning'. The Heber hymn I enjoyed singing most as a boy was 'From Greenland's icy mountains', but I expect it is no longer considered politically correct because it is a stark statement of the conviction that all other religions are 'in error's chain'. The Bishop must surely have been thinking about Hindus when he wrote:

> *The heathen in his blindness,*
> *Bows down to wood and stone. . . .*
> *Can we whose souls are lighted*
> *With wisdom from on high,*
> *Can we to men benighted*
> *The lamp of life deny?*

When the foundation stone of the cathedral was laid in 1847, the spirit of Bishop Heber lived on. God was invoked with this prayer: 'Behold us here surrounded by millions of our fellow-men who know not the name of him by whom alone they can be saved, having their understandings darkened and being sunk into sin and sensuality. In thy goodness then prosper this our undertaking . . . until this land of darkness be illuminated in all its recesses with the light of the everlasting gospel.'

Of course there were some missionaries who realized that Christianity had to make concessions to India. In 1793 the English Baptist William Carey set sail for Bengal. He was to become an outstanding scholar of Indian languages, setting up his own college and printing press at Serampore outside Calcutta. He worked with Indian scholars to translate the Bible into many languages, but he also translated the Hindu Vedas into English so that missionaries could have a better understanding of the religion from which they were attempting to make converts. One of his friends, the Reverend Andrew Fuller, described this project as 'obscene', but Carey believed the translations would help missionaries counter Hindu doctrines. At the same time he was delighted to think that the money made from these translations would be used for printing more Bibles. He wrote back to his friend, 'It makes us smile . . . when we consider that Satan will probably here be overshot in his own bow. He certainly did not intend when he dictated those vile and destructive fables, that the publishing of them to the enlightened world, should supply a fund for circulating the oracles of truth.' So, for Carey too, the sacred writings of Hinduism were vile and only Christianity was true. But he did acknowledge that Hinduism was more than just bowing down to wood and stone. Its teachings needed understanding if they were to be refuted.

Carey's achievements in the field of education have to be admired, as do the schools and hospitals provided by other missionaries. Nor should we judge Carey's or Heber's theology in the light of our times. They were sincere Christians who dedicated their lives to the Jesus of their day.

As a child in India I was brought up to believe in a Jesus quite like theirs. Hinduism was nothing more than idolatry, an abomination because of the second commandment, 'You shall not make for yourself a graven image, or any likeness of anything that is in heaven above, or that is in the earth beneath, or that is in the water under the earth; you shall not bow down to them or serve them; for I, the Lord your God, am a jealous God. . . .' Disgust and fear of idolatry were so ingrained in me that I was almost sick with terror when I caught a glimpse of the gaudy images of the goddess Durga, with her many arms, riding on her tiger, during the festival of Durga, which is Calcutta's version of Christmas. I well remember being taught that Muslims were more acceptable than Hindus because at least they believed in one God and did not worship idols. No one ever suggested to me that God might be at work in any other religion. Now, attitudes are changing. Until recently the Roman Catholic Church insisted that it was the only true Church, and that there was no salvation outside it. But since the Second Vatican Council Catholics have been encouraged to see signs of God's work in those outside the Church, and even in other faiths.

Finding common ground with Hinduism

Over the years I have lived in India as an adult I have come to realize that Christianity actually has a lot in common with Hinduism. In this I am by no means alone, as I discovered when I met again Ursula King, Professor of Religion at Bristol University. I had known her nearly thirty years earlier when she was a student of Western and Indian philosophy in Delhi. In spite of the interval, I recognized her immediately: fair-haired with a round, still young face and a most infectious grin. Clearly years of study had not dimmed her enthusiasm for learning more about comparative religion. Although she had only just arrived after a tiring flight from Britain, she insisted on accompanying me to a service in a village church. The next day, her enthusiasm was really put to the test as we set out to travel from Madras to Trichinopoly, or Tiruchirapalli as it's now known. The conductor of the Vaigai Express told us that the scheduled air-conditioned compartment was 'not available today', and then, looking at our tickets, said, 'Anyhow, you are only on the waiting list.' Rather than being put out, she took a great interest in the complicated negotiations I conducted to persuade the conductor to forget the waiting list and provide us with at least one window seat in a non air-conditioned compartment. Although we were travelling for nearly six hours through the heat of a south Indian summer day, the conversation never faltered. I caught up with her family and learnt a great deal about the current state of theology.

The next morning we drove through the modern gateway which towers over the Sri Ranganathaswami Temple outside Tiruchirapalli. It is one of several magnificent Hindu temples in south India, but those who worship the god Vishnu always refer to it simply as 'the Temple'. Vishnu, the source of the universe and everything in it, lies enthroned on the thousand-hooded serpent of eternity in the inner sanctuary, which is surrounded by seven courtyards. We were able to drive through the outer courtyards with their shops selling fruit, flowers, sweets, coconuts, incense, camphor and every-thing else that pilgrims need for their *puja* or worship. In the fourth courtyard we got out of the car and took off our shoes before entering the northern gate. We had arrived early, before the sun had heated the floor of the temple, to avoid burning the soles of our bare feet. Our guide, P. Soundararajan, knew every inch of the place. He was a journalist who had lived all his life on the island in the River Kaveri that the temple occupies. As we passed a small shrine containing an image of the monkey god Hanuman he said, 'Devotees worship here, then they go on to worship Garuda, king of the birds, before entering the sanctuary of Vishnu. It's like when you go to request some help from a government minister – you pay court to his personal assistants before going in to see the big man himself.'

We entered the hall to see the image of Garuda, and walked through row after row of carved pillars supporting the roof. There were no arches to hold it up, as in the great medieval cathedrals of Britain. One hall in the temple has a thousand pillars. Garuda may be just a minor deity, but I was over-awed by the vast beak-faced copper-coloured idol, draped from the waist down in sixteen metres of hand-woven cloth, who loomed out of the semi-darkness of his sanctuary. This was Vishnu's mount: every Hindu god rides on an animal. I was reminded that the four living creatures of Ezekiel's vision who became the symbols of the Gospels originally drove the wheels of God's chariot. In another corner of the hall stood the temple elephant, chalked on her face a white V with a red line down the middle of it. This is the emblem of Vishnu, and is worn by priests and other devotees on their foreheads. We watched as pilgrims put coins in the tip of her trunk. The elephant would then lift her trunk and touch their heads as a blessing before handing the money to her mahout.

We went out of the hall and climbed on to the roof of a building in the fourth courtyard from where we could see the entire area of the temple, more than a quarter of a square mile. One line of *goparam*, or towers, built over gateways in the walls of the courtyards ran from east to west; another went from north to south. The lines crossed at the golden dome, beneath which Vishnu lay on the eternal serpent. Down below I could see pilgrims stopping to worship at little shrines as they made their way from courtyard to courtyard, destined eventually for the holiest shrine of all. Two brahmins, the front of their heads shaved and a small tuft growing at the back, were carrying copper pots filled with water from the sacred River Kaveri. They must have had difficulty in finding the water, because when I crossed the bridge to the island the wide river-bed seemed nothing but sand: the water upstream had been siphoned off for irrigation. We heard conch shells and drums indicating that the Brahmin priests had finished bathing, dressing and feeding the image in one of the shrines. They would now be drawing back the curtain in front of the shrine so that pilgrims could come forward for a *darshan* or 'sight' of the image. The many gods and goddesses, the shrines, the pilgrims smearing red *sindoor* or paste on their foreheads, the Brahmins with sacred threads running across their bare chests – all seemed utterly alien to Christianity. Yet Ursula King, who is a Roman Catholic, said to me, 'Vishnu is at the centre of this temple and in that central place. It's almost like going into a Catholic Church and finding God hidden in the tabernacle above the altar.'

She compared the towers soaring up into the sky to the spires of Gothic cathedrals pulling the worshippers' minds upwards and giving them a sense of the transcendent, and then went on to say, 'From the outside the temple is very large. But it goes into the very small centre where the God is hidden. It's a secret, sacred place. You have the tower as a sign of transcendence, but at the same time you have also the intimacy of a space so hidden that you really have to go and wait for the audience, the *darshan*, when God is ready to receive you.'

I was reminded of Bishop Heber and his hymn condemning the heathen for bowing down to wood and stone, and told Ursula King how as a child I had been terrified by the images of Durga in Calcutta. But Ursula insisted that nobody really worships wood and stones. She explained, 'The worshipper worships *through* the images. The images are a mere sign to point to something which is ultimately invisible. When a worshipper has a *darshan* of the image, he or she is getting in touch, having an audience with the god. The images are just a manifestation.'

Ursula went on to suggest that the concept of God being in the image might have some parallel with the Catholic belief that Christ is literally present in the consecrated host, which can be worshipped physically in the reserved sacrament, 'They are both pointing to a particular space where the power of the sacred is concentrated,' she said.

One of the most common mistakes made by traditional Christians is to believe that Hinduism must be in error because it has many gods. In the West this has been called polytheism, and has always been considered inferior to monotheism, the worship of one God. But the truth is that Hindus are not really polytheists. They worship one God in many different manifestations. Even when it comes to understanding those many manifestations, there are unexpected parallels with Christianity. Christians revere saints and holy people, lighting candles in their honour and sometimes praying to them. When Christianity came to Britain, local gods were sometimes transformed into Christian saints. Christians also call on angels and archangels to worship with them and protect them. Many believe in personal or guardian angels. It is a common practice in almost all churches to stress different aspects of God at different times and seasons: at Pentecost Christians worship God as the Holy Spirit, on Trinity Sunday God as the three in one, and at Christmas God manifested in the baby Jesus.

To Ursula King the temple with its different shrines, its many pillars, its towers and courtyards, embodied the myriad forms of the one God. Although in Hinduism there is not just one way of worshipping God, she explained, 'All ways point to the one, the hidden and unmanifest, which expresses itself in a myriad of forms. The strength of Hinduism is its diversity. But this very strength is its weakness too, because it gets so diffused. In Christianity the strength is the concentration, and the one-pointedness, but the problem with that is that it cuts out a lot of the differences, and the richness.'

Perhaps the form of Hindu worship which is easiest for Christians to understand is devotion to a personal God believed to have lived on Earth. My father was a devout Christian, but when I was still at school he gave me a copy of the *Bhagavad Gita*, which means *The Song of the Lord*. It forms part of the great epic the *Mahabharata*, relating the conversation between the Hindu god Krishna and the reluctant warrior Arjuna. Krishna is one of the incarnations of Vishnu, and in the *Bhagavad Gita* he explains why God comes down to Earth from time to time: 'Whenever there is a decline of righteousness and rise of uprighteousness then I send forth myself. For the protection of the good, for the destruction of the wicked, and for the establishment of righteousness, I come into being from age to age.'

This is the Hindu version of the incarnation – God coming to Earth to save mankind from folly and destruction. The copy of the *Bhagavad Gita* that my father gave me was a translation by Christopher Isherwood and a Hindu scholar named Swami Prabhavananda. In their introduction they describe the *Gita* as a gospel, saying, 'Its essential message is timeless. In words which belong to no one language, race or epoch, incarnate God speaks to man his friend.'

There are, of course, many differences between Hindu incarnations of God and the Christian belief in the divinity of Jesus. Vaishnavites, for instance, believe that there have been nine incarnations of Vishnu and that there is a tenth still to come. Vishnu is able to change his earthly form at will, while his divine being remains constant. In contrast, Christianity insists that the incarnation has only happened once, and that the man, Jesus of Nazareth, is the permanent human form of God. Without Jesus there is no Christianity, and Christians have to acknowledge that their incarnation was not only a historical figure, but also the one and only time that God came down and lived among us. We are back to the problem of the uniqueness of Jesus, which Christianity can never let go. The diversity of Hinduism means you can express devotion to the incarnate Krishna, or not, as you like. You can also accept him as either a historical or a mythological figure.

Yet, for me, both Jesus and Krishna are attractive for the same reason. A God who is also human is a God who can be loved, who can be relied on, who can be a companion through life. He can be as close and loving to us as we can be to each other. It is much easier to feel close to Jesus than to the remote God on high of the Old Testament. It is much easier to feel close to Krishna playing his flute than it is to Vishnu lying on his thousand-hooded serpent. Ursula King described Krishna to me as 'the approachable God'.

Krishna standing on the fire-breathing serpent king, Kaliya, who laid waste to all around him. Krishna defeated him and banished him from the earth. Krishna is revered as the eighth incarnation of the god Vishnu, the source of all existence and giver of law. Krishna's exploits are celebrated in Hindu mythology. Sixteenth-century statue from Madras.

The qualities of personal gods, their divinity and their humanity, are illustrated for believers in their birth stories. Ursula King pointed out that there were parallels between the Nativity of Jesus and the Nativity of Krishna. Krishna's was no ordinary conception. Like Jesus he was born of both God and a mortal woman. In the Krishna stories, Vishnu implanted one of his hairs in the womb of Krishna's mother. His earthly parents fled from the wicked tyrant Kamsa, just as Joseph and Mary fled from Herod in St Matthew's Gospel. Both rulers came to know of the divine incarnation and did their best to kill the babies. Both births were surrounded by miraculous events. This medieval poem, describes the birth of Krishna:

> I've hurried over, for the news has come:
> Yashoda's a mother, given birth to a son.
> The courtyard throbs with songs of acclaim,
> And what am I to say at sight of such a scene?
> Jewels strewn thick cover the earth;
> Everyone's dancing, from aged to infants;
> The air is stirred in a swirl of dirt and curds;
> Cow-herds and herds-women crowd at the door
> With even more praises – what am I to say?
> Surdas' Lord is the one who knows each mood
> And gives the world its joy – as Nanda's little boy.

The poem reminds me of Christmas carols. In both there is 'joy to the world', and a contrast between divine richness and human poverty. I am tempted to substitute the shepherds of St Luke's Gospel for cow-herds and herds-women.

Ursula King said, 'I think you have to compare the birth of heroes and divine figures in a number of religions and you get a similar kind of pattern. The birth of the Buddha was also accompanied by signs and wonders. It is a way of marking the extra-ordinariness, the breaking of all boundaries, so that within the human there is more than what is human. There's a kind of revelation which is captured at this moment of time in this particular figure.' She told me the delightful story about the child Krishna playing with mud. His foster-mother said, 'Open your mouth. You've eaten some of the mud.' Krishna denied that, but his foster-mother insisted, 'You have! Open your mouth.' So Krishna did, and his foster-mother saw the entire universe inside it. Terrified, she pleaded with him to be a normal child. There was, I thought, perhaps a parallel there with St Luke's story of the boy Jesus slipping away from his parents to teach the teachers of the law in the Temple of Jerusalem. His mother Mary, instead of being proud that 'all who heard him were amazed at his understanding and his answers', reprimanded him for getting lost and causing her and Joseph so much trouble.

I asked Ursula King how she could reconcile the parallels she found between Hinduism and Christianity with the Christian creed which says, 'I believe in one God the Father Almighty, and in Jesus Christ his only Son our Lord, who was conceived by the Holy Ghost and born of the Virgin Mary.'

She replied, 'That's a theological claim which one has to interpret and understand. In the West we have this very rationalistic approach. We insist that Jesus is either everything or nothing. But the Eastern approach, the Indian approach, is much more inclusive. We can accept Jesus, but we can also accept Krishna.'

'But surely there is a difference?' I replied, 'Christians *have* to believe the divine Jesus was a historical figure. Hindus can simply accept Krishna as a mythical figure, can't they?'

'Well, Mark, that's just a perfect example of an either/or. *Either* it's alleged in myth *or* it's history. I find that much too one-dimensional. You see, Krishna is as real to the Hindu as Christ is to the Christian. It's the reality of the experience, the reality of the psychological impact that counts. History as history doesn't mean anything if it doesn't set an example, if it doesn't inspire, if it doesn't transform the self and the world.' In other words, history has to connect with your own experience if it is to mean anything to you. I thought of Richard Burridge and his insistence that facts alone cannot bring you to truth – only the interpretation of them.

My conversation with Ursula reminded me of an Indian Jesuit I had once met who had told me that, although he had spent some fifteen years engaged in rigorous study of Christian theology, and although his family had been Christian for four generations, Krishna still meant more to him than Jesus. Having spent so much time in India, I find that I share his feeling. In some ways Krishna has come to mean more to me than Jesus. My difficulty had always been that the incarnation did not give me a Jesus I could talk to, as Arjuna did to Krishna. I admired the teachings of the human Jesus, and admired his life in which he lived out the great commandments. He really did love the Lord his God, and his neighbour as himself. But I still found him a

Baby Krishna (LEFT) and baby Jesus. Both Hinduism and Christianity have
a rich mythology of the child-god, whose human vulnerability evokes
devotion and yet is wise beyond his years. The detail of Jesus comes
from Fra Angelico's *Madonna and Child with Eight Saints*, 1450.

distant figure who had set an example it was impossible to follow. The more I tried, the more I was aware of my own inadequacy. I suppose the only way I could put it would be to say I was not able to internalize the forgiveness I was told had been won for me by Jesus's Crucifixion. As a student, I drowned the pain of this guilt in drink. As I grew older, I overcame it by bothering less and less about sin.

In India I began to think of a different way of understanding God. From Hinduism I came to learn that there was not such a great gap between me and God. The divine was in all of us. As the Cambridge scholar Julius Lipner has put it, 'The deity is one's antar-atma, one's inner self.' Hinduism is, of course, not monochrome. It is a many-splendoured religion, which acknowledges different levels of spiritual achievement and different paths to salvation. We are all, though, moving towards the same destination, which Lipner describes as, 'Dissolving the individual ego ... and realising that in spirit we are identical with Brahman, the ultimate reality.' I began to wonder whether the meaning of Jesus's divinity might be that he was one man who had truly dissolved his own ego and fully realized his identity with God. I found this particularly attractive because I knew that for me the enemy of 'that peace which passeth all understanding' was the ego, the grasping selfishness which has us all in its grip. I found it easy to understand why I should try to resist the call of my ego, because when I did I was happy and when I did not I made myself unhappy. It was as simple as that. What is more, I came to regard my frequent failures to curb my ego as stupidity, not sin. I was not inherently evil, needing a divine forgiveness I couldn't bring myself to believe in. I was foolish, which I found much easier to live with, not least because it held out the possibility of improvement.

Sai Baba: god-man?

This concept of the divine in all of us seems to appeal to an increasing number of people brought up as Christians. Outside Bangalore, the fast expanding hi-tech capital of India, there is a religious centre of Sri Sathya Sai Baba, who is one of the best-known modern god-men. There I found thousands of people who believed that Sai Baba was an incarnation of God. He maintains that we are divine. The only difference between him and us is that he recognizes the fact while the rest of us do not.

The complex at Whitefields is a vast ashram where Sai Baba lives for part of the year. It has a college, large hostels and permanent accommodation for some of those who have given their lives to following the guru. In the centre of the courtyard is a hall open on three sides, where devotees gather at eight o'clock in the morning for a *darshan*, or audience, with the man they believe is God. Sitting cross-legged on the floor, waiting for the daily *darshan*, I looked around at the congregation. The hall could seat five thousand and yet, that morning at least, there were plenty of devotees who had to sit outside in the sun. I noticed that there were many foreigners among the congregation. On one side of me a middle-aged Indian, well dressed and obviously comparatively prosperous, was reciting mantas or sacred verses. On the other side a young man who could have come from Europe or America was quietly writing in a notebook. In front of me there were rows of neat young students from the college. The women sat across the aisle, separated from the men. The foreigners among them, like the Indians, were dressed in saris or *salvar qamiz* – long shirts with baggy trousers. All the women had covered their shoulders with scarves. The Indians and foreigners seemed to be part of the mainstream of life. I could see no sign of new-agers or others who had chosen alternative lifestyles.

Ushers made sure that everyone sat in neat blocks, leaving room for Sai Baba to walk between them. A woman put the finishing touches to the arrangement of red roses and white jasmine which adorned an image of Ganesh, the elephant god. Other women dusted and swabbed the floor to make sure the hall was spotless. This congregation was as silent and orderly as any in a church. It was very different from the Sri Ranganathaswami Temple, where everyone seemed to be doing their own thing.

Suddenly all heads turned as a diminutive figure with a mop of frizzy black hair emerged through a gate and walked over to a group of women sitting outside. He greeted them and then stepped into the hall. I could see now that Sai Baba was very small indeed, and very thin. He was wearing a flowing

OVERLEAF
Sai Baba is one of India's best-known and most
popular god-men. He is regarded as an avatar, or
incarnation, by his devotees. They credit
him with miraculous powers.

saffron tunic, so long that the cloth trailed along the floor as he strolled around the hall lifting his hands in blessing. From time to time he stopped and spoke briefly to someone, or received a petition in an envelope. Some fell at the god's feet as he passed by. I was one of the lucky ones: Sai Baba touched me on the forehead. I looked closely at him but I really could not tell his age. He was reported to be seventy.

Eventually Sai Baba made his way to a throne in the front of the hall, flanked by life-sized pictures of him. When he was seated the sound of a long drawn out 'ohmm . . .' rose from the congregation. *Aum*, as it is spelt, is a mantra, one of a number of Hindu sacred words or verses. Sai Baba's followers describe *aum* as 'the mystic monosyllable representing the deity, the sound of the universe; the sound of divinity, the sound of creation'. Twice more the congregation intoned 'ohmm . . .', and then started singing *bhajans* – hymns – accompanied by harmoniums and drums. Sai Baba sat there smiling beatifically, waving his hand gently in time with the music. One of the recorded *bhajan*s on sale in praise of Sai Baba describes him as:

> *Our Mother, Father, Sister and Brother all in one.*
> *The earth, fire, water, moon and the sun.*

When the *bhajan*s were over Sai Baba left the hall. Throughout the *darshan* he had not said a word to the congregation. He had neither preached, nor taught. His devotees had not expected that. Their only aim had been to look into the eyes of Sai Baba, to have their *darshan*.

Outside in the courtyard I asked a woman who was a Christian how Sai Baba had taught her to regard the divinity of Jesus. She replied, 'Swami says there are stages. In the first stage you are a messenger of God, you realize that you are divine. The second stage is that you are becoming the son of God – or daughter of God in my case. That means you come closer and you already feel the oneness there. And the third stage is your real life, the recognition that you are God. Jesus was realizing that at the end of his life. I'm sure that he is one with the Father.' I asked another woman who had given up a good job in London to come and live as a follower of Sai Baba whether she thought he was as much God as Jesus was. She replied, 'I think we're all as much God as Jesus was God. You are as much God as Jesus was, and so am I.'

'So what's the difference between us and Jesus or Sai Baba?'

'That they know it and we don't.'

I met a group of Iranians who said, 'Don't interview us – we will be in real trouble if it's known in our country that we are devotees of Sai Baba.' An American told me he believed in Krishna, Shiva, Jesus and Sai Baba. An Austrian was less certain that Sai Baba was God, but he did regard him as illuminated. His daughter was struck by Sai Baba's belief that all religions were ways to God. She said, 'In my country there is only one Catholic Church and this Church says we know the truth – the only truth. My Church has a Pope and a great organization behind it which sends missionaries to other countries and says you have to believe in Christ. But I'm not sure that this is what I think religion is really about.' Apparently the thinking of modern Catholic theologians like Ursula King had not penetrated the Roman Catholic Church in Austria. It was still teaching the absolute superiority of Christianity, and the utter uniqueness of God's once-for-all incarnation, excluding any insights that might come through other faiths.

I was reminded of Ursula King when I found that the legends which have grown up around Sai Baba had their own parallels with the Gospel stories. His mother said Sai Baba had been miraculously conceived when she was standing at a well and a great light entered her. The birth was accompanied by miraculous signs: musical instruments played without any musicians. Sai Baba was born into a humble home. Astrologers say that the stars had predicted the birth of an incarnation of God. As a young boy he was precocious, like Jesus in the Temple. There were those who said the devil had entered into him, which is what some thought of Jesus. According to an authorized biography an exorcist was summoned who shaved the young Sai Baba's head, made cuts in his scalp and squeezed lime into them. When he showed no sign of pain, the exorcist rubbed the cuts with red chillies and even poured acid into them. Sai Baba was also beaten with a stick and doused daily with one hundred and eight buckets of cold water. When none of these desperate measures succeeded in driving out the devil, the exorcist rubbed into his eyes a paste which caused Sai Baba's face to swell. At last he showed signs of feeling pain, and wept. His parents became alarmed but Sai Baba told them where they could get a herb which would relieve the pain. The remedy worked and the exorcist was dismissed.

Like Jesus, too, Sai Baba was and still is credited with healing and other miracles. Some of these miracles, particularly his practice of producing sacred ash and other more mundane objects, like rings, out of thin air, have led to allegations that he is a charlatan, nothing more than a conjurer. But at Whitefields I met a retired civil servant who is now a renowned artist, a most sane and reasonable man, who believed he had witnessed a miracle. When he asked Sai Baba about the controversies surrounding his miracles Sai Baba replied, 'There isn't anything in them to be troubled about. They are transient, like passing clouds.' He then made a few circular movements with his right hand and in it appeared a ring, which he gave to the civil servant.

It would be a mistake to think that devotees are attracted to Sai Baba just because they believe he performs miracles. It would be a similar mistake to think that it was only his reputation as a crowd-pulling wonder-worker which inspired the followers of Jesus. More is going on, and real faith can survive disappointment. At Whitefields I met V. K. Narasimhan, formerly one of India's leading journalists. During the 'state of emergency' which Indira Gandhi imposed from 1975 to 1977, when some journalists were imprisoned for breaking the rigorous censorship, Narasimhan edited the *Indian Express*, one of the few papers which had the courage to defy the censors. Narasimhan had first come to Sai Baba because his grandson's brain was damaged, and he hoped for a miraculous cure. Although his grandson died Narasimhan dedicated the rest of his life to Sai Baba, settling down at Whitefields and editing the movement's magazine. When I asked Narasimhan why he was so dedicated to Sai Baba he replied, 'There is something Christ-like about him.'

I only saw Sai Baba at two of his *darshan*s. I never got the chance to talk to him, but I did read some of his writings. I cannot say they made a deep impact on me, but with my very limited reading, experience and understanding it would be quite improper for me to pass judgement on Sai Baba's claim to divinity. What I do accept wholeheartedly is that belief in Sai Baba, which has spread to more than one hundred and thirty countries, demonstrates how strong the desire still is for a God who can understand us because he has lived on this earth or indeed does still live here. We are drawn to the idea of a God who has come down from that remote Heaven and who is less remote than the ultimate reality, which in Hinduism is called Brahman. If that desire is still so strong in these sceptical days, it is easy to understand its force in Jesus's time when the existence of God was taken for granted by the vast majority of people.

So where does all this leave the Christians of India, some of whom trace their faith back to the Apostle Thomas? India is a land of many incarnations, but Indian Christians are still taught that Jesus is the only true incarnation of God. That was the message of the missionaries, and that is still the message of the three largest Churches: the Roman Catholic Church and the Churches of North and South India. These latter two Churches were formed when the Anglican Church in India united with the main Protestant Churches after independence.

Christianity and the Dalits

Most of those whom the missionaries converted were 'untouchables' – people outside the caste system who suffered discrimination and oppression in Indian society. They now choose to be called Dalits or 'the oppressed'. Bishop Azariah is the first Dalit Christian to be the leader of the important Church of South India diocese of Madras. He is widely respected among Dalit Christians of all denominations for his stand against the discrimination they still suffer, even in the Churches.

The Bishop embraced me warmly when we met in the coastal fishing village of Covelong, south of Madras. It was not the first time I had encountered him. A bouncy, handsome man with curly grey hair and a friendly face, usually creased by a broad smile, he was wearing a spotless white cassock with a simple wooden pectoral cross. The smile disappeared from his face when I asked whether the uniqueness of Jesus really mattered to Indian Christians. He replied with all the majesty of his office, 'The assertion that Christianity is the one true faith is not just a claim made by Christians. Jesus asserted it himself when he said, "I am the Way, the Truth and the Life". I don't have to convince my people of that – they discover that Jesus is the only God because they are able to communicate with him, pray to him and listen to him.'

Bishop Azariah told me how, as a young child, he would wake up and hear his mother, who had no education, talking aloud to someone. He used to sit up and look around to see who she was talking to and then realize that that person was Jesus. He explained, 'There I could see the reality of Christ as one who is experienced both as a human person as well as divine.'

The Bishop drew a sharp dividing line between Jesus and the Indian avatars. The Indian gods, he said, came and went; their human form dissolved as they returned to pure divinity. In contrast, he said, Jesus continued to be human through his death and Resurrection, and still continues to be human because of the relationship he has with us.

I noticed that Bishop Azariah seemed to have no difficulty in combining Jesus the friend with a very different Jesus, the political liberator, who was on the side of the Dalits in their struggle for equality. I admired the Bishop's commitment to the Dalit cause, but my knowledge of their situation prompted me to suggest that the Jesus of the missionaries had not, in fact, liberated the Dalit Christians. In India, most Christians retain their caste identity. In spite of their conversion to the egalitarian religion of Christianity Dalits were still sometimes segregated from others in church, discouraged from reading lessons or taking a prominent part in services, and even buried in separate graveyards from the Christians of higher castes. All this went on in the Bishop's own state of Tamil Nadu. When I pointed this out to him he did not deny it, but he defended the missionaries and the orthodox Christianity they had taught saying, 'What you claim about the failure of the missionaries is not really true. Dalits suffer lack of dignity and self-respect because of the shame and stigma of their birth. I can overcome that shame because Jesus is a liberator. The idea that the kingdom of God is coming, as preached by Jesus, gives Dalit Christians the hope for change too. Liberation is what they were able to see in this message of salvation.'

Although Bishop Azariah is a leader of the Church of South India, most of Covelong's Christians are Roman Catholics. After he left I met a remarkable Dalit Catholic, Arokia Mary, which means Our Lady of Health. Young and extraordinarily energetic, she cycled miles every day undertaking her duties of instructing children in the faith. She was the only woman catechist in the Madras diocese. Although about thirty, she was still unmarried, which is very unusual in a community like hers. She lived with her parents and relatives in a cluster of small mud huts thatched with dried palm leaves. I noticed that instead of the cross I had expected, a small silver pistol hung from her necklace. When I asked why she roared with laughter and said, 'To shoot the high-caste people.' The church in the village had been built in 1808, which meant the Roman Catholic missionaries had arrived there nearly two hundred years ago, yet Dalit Christians like Arokia Mary obviously still felt they had not been liberated from the discrimination and humiliation imposed on them by the Hindu caste system. Still, she was not disheartened. When I asked her whether she thought that Jesus identified with the Dalits she replied, 'Yes, of course he *is* a Dalit. That's why I'm very happy.'

'But what has Jesus done for your community since they became Christians?'

'He is on our side. I'm very close to Jesus and so I know. Because he's on our side I'm very happy to be a Dalit.'

It was Maundy Thursday and Mary suggested that I should attend the service that evening. The church was packed with women and children, and I stood in the porch with the men. Everyone living in the Christian quarter of the village seemed to be there. In the sandy square outside the church there were only cows asleep under the rain trees and the occasional desultory dog wandering around. The moon rose blood-red from the Bay of Bengal, and cut a silver path through the clouds. An owl screeched. The murmur of the sea could be heard as the congregation waited in silence for the service to start. Eventually a young bearded priest wearing red vestments walked out of the vestry, accompanied by four or five altar boys. As he moved to his place behind the altar I noticed that on the arch separating the chancel from the body of the church there was a painting of a very Western-looking Jesus. Father Niddi celebrated the mass in Tamil, the language of the villagers, but I had no difficulty in following it because the form was traditional and familiar to anyone brought up as a Christian in the West. Neither in the imagery nor in the ritual was there any sign of Mary's Dalit Jesus, or indeed any kind of Indian Jesus.

The search for an Indian Jesus

There are many Indian Christians who feel that an Indianized Jesus is necessary if he is to be a God who is relevant to those whose civilization is so ancient and so different from that of the West. Theologians have coined the rather ugly word 'adaptionists' for those Protestants and Catholics who try to bring India into Christianity. Jyoti Sahi, an internationally acclaimed Indian Christian artist, is one of them. He has written, 'Ultimately the purpose of art is to reveal to the worshipper what HE is. That is why we want an Indian Christian art. A foreign art cannot reveal to the Indian what HE is.'

I met Jyoti Sahi at his artists' ashram in the village of Silvepura, about forty minutes' drive from Bangalore. It was a collection of small cottages in a grove;

in the centre was a gallery covered with purple and white bougainvillea, and in one corner a small chapel designed like a mandala, a sacred Hindu pattern. The artist himself was lean and ascetic-looking, bespectacled, with a fine head of long grey hair and a bushy black beard, grey on the cheeks. I was struck by the variety of the style of the paintings he showed me. There were swirling lines creating distorted faces. One long face with deep-set eyes reminded me of El Greco. There was a face which recalled Blake's *Ancient of Days*. A painting of Jesus crucified seemed to have been influenced by Gauguin's *Yellow Christ*. Thin, matchstick figures came from one of the traditions of Indian tribal art. Jyoti Sahi told me he had painted the Stations of the Cross with Jesus in yoga positions. He had produced a crucifix with Jesus depicted like the god Shiva, dancing the creation of the world. He had also depicted the infant Jesus in a way that resembled the infant Krishna.

Jyoti Sahi's art had not always met with the Church's approval. He had been told that some paintings were too Hindu and one had contained 'too much nudity'. This criticism had caused him considerable pain because he regarded himself as 'orthodox, if not thoroughly orthodox', and valued his reputation as 'a theologian recognized by the Church' as well as an artist. He told me that he had taught himself theology. Orthodox though he claimed to be, he still insisted that Jesus must in some way be related to the reality of India and he continued to represent Jesus in Indian contexts so that the people of his country could find a version of Jesus who spoke to them.

Jyoti's mother was English, but his father was Indian and Hindu. When he was fourteen his mother had become a Roman Catholic and this had caused tension for both of them. They realized the power of his father's Indian spiritual tradition but could not see how that could be linked with their Christianity. Eventually Jyoti saw a way to do this through what he called 'the ocean of myths', which he regarded as the most important aspect of Indian religion. He explained how the myth of the River Ganges descending from the head of the god Shiva had signified to him a divine energy which came down to Earth. He had also painted for a German church a picture based on the

The mass of Maundy Thursday attended by Mark Tully and
Arokia Mary in the Dalit village of Covelong, south of Madras.
The priests wear red to signify the Passion of Christ.

descent of the Ganges which he linked with the story of Jesus asking the woman of Samaria to give him a drink from a well. This story, in St John's Gospel, has Jesus saying, 'Whoever drinks of the water that I shall give him will never thirst; the water that I shall give him will become in him a spring of water welling up to eternal life.'

Jyoti went on to say, 'I think that in the West much of the real energy and power of religious experience has got lost because we've thrown out the myths and symbols and become over-rational. Lots of young people find going to church very meaningless. I don't think that means they are not religious or that they are not, as much as at any time, searching for something spiritual. They want to find something which links them back to these very powerful images and stories which have somehow been pushed into the unconscious. The attraction for people in the West of Eastern religions is that they find they can rediscover these myths and symbols.'

But was the belief that Jesus was human and divine built on a myth? Jyoti accepted that the birth and Resurrection stories may have been what he called 'legendary in character', and probably represented the meaning Jesus came to have for the Church. So what, I wondered, was the difference between the mythical Jesus and the mythical Krishna? Jyoti had a very interesting answer to that. He believed the main difference was that stories were told about Krishna whereas Jesus himself told stories. To him, the historical Jesus was primarily a story-teller. His own artistic work was inspired by those stories and what they told him about Jesus. He went on to remind me that Mahatma Gandhi had once said that, even if Jesus had not existed, he would still revere him for his sayings.

Jyoti did believe that there were other important differences between Jesus and the Indian gods. Jesus was a God who came from below, from a genuinely poor family, whereas, if you looked deeper into stories like the nativity of Krishna, you found that, in spite of his humble upbringing, the Hindu gods were related to kings and rulers. The other thing he found crucial about Jesus was that he was a God who suffered. In fact to Jyoti the essence of the Gospels was the suffering of Jesus. The great figures of Indian religion had taught their

Woodcut in which Jyoti Sahi portrays Jesus as a tribal drummer, dancing the creation into being.

followers to avoid suffering, whereas in the Gospels suffering was seen as a very positive part of the creative process, a stage on the journey to a greater experience of joy.

There are Christians who have gone beyond Jyoti Sahi in their search for an Indian Jesus. One of the best known was Bede Griffiths, a Welsh Roman Catholic monk, who was born in 1906 and died in 1993. He founded a small ashram on the banks of the River Kavari about thirty miles from the Sri Ranganathaswami Temple. Bede Griffiths once explained why he left his Benedictine monastery in Britain to study Indian religion: 'I had begun to find that there was something lacking not only in the Western world but in the Western Church. We were living from one half of our soul, from the conscious rational level, and we needed to discover the other half, the unconscious intuitive dimension.' The title of the book he wrote after more than twenty-eight years in India summed up his belief that we should be moving towards *The Marriage of East and West.*

I never met Bede Griffiths, but I was shown round the ashram by Father Christadas, a monk from the south Indian state of Kerala. He showed me the small hut in which Father Bede had lived, and the ancient typewriter on which he had produced the manuscripts of his books. He showed me where Bede Griffiths was buried – a simple grave with a picture of his face set in the tombstone. He showed me the chapel with its bright, multi-coloured dome. From a distance it looked like the dome of a Hindu temple. When I got nearer I saw that on top of the dome was a statue of Jesus looking like an Indian yogi; below him was St Peter. Father Christadas himself looked like a Hindu holy man, wearing a saffron *lungi* or cloth tied round his waist, and beads round his neck. He had become a disciple of Bede Griffiths at a young age and was now in his mid-forties, youthful-looking and full of restless energy. When I asked him how as a monk of the Benedictine order he could adopt so many of the outward signs of Hinduism, he replied, 'I could see in the light of Christ the greatness of my country's religion. I am not losing anything from Christ by accepting Hinduism. Since I am an Indian I don't want to lose my identity, and the Christian heritage doesn't exclude me from practising my rich Indian heritage.'

Father Bede incorporated a great deal of the rich Indian heritage in his theology. Before he came to India he knew the Hindu doctrine that a balance of male and female forces pervades all creation. He had also come to accept

Jung's teaching that there is a male and a female side to all our natures. What he realized in India was that Western thought and religion were dominated by the male forces. We gave too much importance to reason, to activity, to aggressively serving our egos. He described people in the West as 'each shut-up in his own ego'. Bede Griffiths found that in India the female side of our natures dominated thought and life. Indians emphasized instinct rather than reason, and the passive rather than the active. The future of the world depended, he believed, on the reunification of these two halves of ourselves.

Bede Griffiths also delighted in the Indian attitude towards nature, towards the universe. He wrote of the 'extraordinary sacredness which attaches to every created thing in India'. He explained how earth, water, air, fire, trees, plants and animals are all regarded as sacred in India. Man is sacred too. As I have come to understand it, Indian religions produce a sense of the immanence of the divine power in all nature, and from there you come to realize that this power is also above and beyond nature, transcendent. Bede Griffiths contrasted this with the way that Semitic religions think of God. For Judaism, Islam and Christianity God is 'the transcendent Lord of creation, infinitely holy, that is separate and above nature, and never to be confused with it'.

The West starts from estrangement, the East from familiarity. The West starts from dogma taught from outside, the East from the inner conviction that there is a God. I remember first having this sense of God being simply *there* in the remoteness of the Derbyshire hills. It was an experience of the world being 'charged with the grandeur of God', as the poet Gerard Manley Hopkins wrote.

Bede Griffiths remained a Benedictine monk to his last day – he did not forsake Christianity for an Indian religion. So where did Jesus fit into Bede Griffiths' scheme of things? How could a God who had briefly lived on Earth and then returned to a transcendent Heaven be present in all nature to this day? Myth seemed to be the answer for Bede Griffiths as well as Jyoti Sahi. Bede Griffiths believed that the story of the redemption of mankind through Jesus's life, death and Resurrection was a sacred myth. In his writings he gave what for me was a very meaningful explanation of myth. Far from being a lie, myth is 'the nearest to Truth that we can come'.

Beyond reason

As far as I know, all religions believe that reason can only take us so far, that we have to go beyond it to experience God. Myth has always been a way of getting nearer to describing that experience than any merely factual or coldly rational statement can. As Richard Burridge had said in Wells, the explicit statements of Jesus's divinity in the Gospel of John may not go back to Jesus himself, but they express 'A truer Truth than facts can ever give'.

Bede Griffiths acknowledged that Jesus was a historical figure, not a mythological hero. The myth lay in the interpretation of his life, because that was not amenable to scientific or purely rational description. Bede Griffiths maintained that the myth of Jesus could bring us to understand what he believed was our destiny: to be reunited both with nature and with God. Explaining the divinity of Jesus, he wrote, 'In the depth of his spirit, in that ground or centre of the soul, which exists in every man, he knew himself as one with that ultimate reality which he called God and he experienced himself in this ground of his being in the relationship of a father to a son.' That reality, of course, underlies all nature, all creation, not just man. Bede Griffiths' description of the divinity of Jesus has always seemed to me remarkably close to the Hindu concept of recognizing the divine in ourselves.

Father Christadas told me that the worship in the ashram was an attempt to realize Bede Griffiths' hope of a *Marriage of East and West*. He invited me to attend the midday prayers. As I sat cross-legged on the floor of that Christian chapel listening to the murmuring of *Aum*, a sound which I had last heard in Sai Baba's ashram, I thought to myself, 'How comfortable I have come to feel with Hindu worship, which in my childhood seemed so terrifying.' The dogma I was taught as a Western Christian had not worked for me. It had not given me that inner conviction without which no religion can be anything more than a sham. It was India which had shown me that, although man searches for God in different ways, the search is always for the same God. It was that realization of what I call 'the universal appetite for God' which turned me from someone who hoped God existed to someone who was convinced he did, even though I was still a long way from finding enough effort. It was India which had shown me a God far wider than the narrow figure, obsessed with my sins, that I had created from my Christian education. It was India which had taught me the importance of intuition, as against the acceptance of dry dogma.

There were Christian prayers and readings during the service but it ended with Father Christadas going into the sanctuary, a small dark recess just like the sanctuaries which housed the images in the Sriranganathaswami temple, and circling a lamp filled with burning camphor in front of the blessed sacrament. It was the Hindu sacrament of *arthi*, a symbol of the sacredness of light in Hinduism. To Father Christadas it was a gesture of reverence for Christ the light of the world.

There, I thought, is the problem. Christ the light of the world means Jesus the unique incarnation of God. Hindus are not unduly concerned whether Krishna was a historical figure or not. Followers of Sai Baba believe he is divine, but they do not think he is the only avatar or incarnation who has ever lived. Yet if Christians cease to believe that the historical Jesus was a unique incarnation, in some sense the only incarnation, the belief that Jesus is God will not survive the next millennium. Had Bede Griffiths crossed the boundary of Richard Burridge's ball park? What are the limits that history sets on Jesus? The Gospels themselves suggest that this is the key question. The fact that the Gospels appear to be written in the genre of other ancient biographies suggests that the writers wanted to present Jesus as a human figure, a man of his times, as solidly historical as Agricola or any other significant figure of the ancient world. The Gospel writers did not see Jesus simply as a God who came down from Heaven. It was his actual human life, and terrible death, which revealed his divinity. What was it about that human life which was so remarkable? To discover that we have to study not Jesus the God, but Jesus the man.

2

Jesus the Jew

Who was Jesus?

I can think of no less suitable place to start a journey of a lifetime than
London's Heathrow Airport. I have always wanted to go to the Holy
Land, which is what I was brought up to call the territory which now
comprises Israel and the surrounding Arab states. I wanted to go there
because it is the land of the New Testament, which has had a more profound
influence on me than other literature. It is also the birthplace of the Church,
an institution which has fascinated me from childhood. Because the Holy
Land means so much to me I would like to have arrived there by land or sea,
crossing the border or landing at a port with a sense of a journey accomplished. There is no romance in air travel. But at least El Al, Israel's national
airline, does relieve the monotony of those dreary airport departures. Before
passengers are allowed to board they are grilled by skilled security officers as
though they were suspects being interrogated in a police station. A young lady
asked me whether I had ever been to Israel before.

'No,' I answered with confidence.

'Are you sure?' she shot back.

I suddenly remembered I had once transited through Tel Aviv Airport.
Should I confess to that? 'Are you sure?' she repeated.

'Well, I did once pass through one of your airports,' I said.

'That doesn't count if you didn't go through immigration,' she replied
brusquely, and went on to ask whether I knew anyone in Israel.

I do have some Israeli friends, but I was becoming so nervous that I was
worried they would be in difficulties if I revealed their names. I half expected
her to search my contact book and find them. I bought time by explaining that

I was a journalist who had worked in India for many years and that at least two of my fellow correspondents were now posted in Israel. Israeli security must, I thought, know about them, and surely there could be nothing wrong in their having journalist friends.

My interrogator went off on another track. Was I going to Israel on holiday or to work? Surrounded as I was by a mountain of camera equipment and a complete BBC television crew, I could hardly deny I was going to work. So I explained my mission. Then I panicked again. The mention of Jesus might make her think I was a Christian linked to those Churches which have made no secret of their pro-Palestinian sympathies. But by now my interrogator had become thoroughly confused herself.

'You work in India and you have been chosen to present these documentaries about Jesus? Why you?' she asked in amazement.

I could only think of trying to laugh my way out of the corner she had boxed me into, so I said, 'Well, there are those who believe that Jesus died in India. There is even a tomb in Kashmir where he's believed to be buried.'

My interrogator looked at me with incredulity, and then, presumably thinking that someone gullible enough to believe that could not represent any sort of security threat to the state of Israel, she burst into laughter, saying, 'Why don't you say you've been chosen because you are the best person for the job?' I mumbled something about not being at all sure I was, and she dismissed me.

As I waited to board the plane I thought about the modern role of Christianity in Israel. I knew that, although Israel was the land where Jesus was born, lived his whole life and died, Christians were now a very small minority. Most of them were Palestinians belonging to the ancient Eastern Churches, and were not particularly welcome to the Israeli authorities. In fact they found themselves treated with suspicion by the Israelis and their fellow Arabs who were Muslims. Around me I could see the Christians who were made welcome by the Israel Government – two parties of Christian pilgrims, part of a very lucrative tourist trade.

The impression that it was Islam and Judaism, not Christianity, which counted in Israel now was confirmed when I reached Jerusalem, the three thousand-year-old city of the great King David. Jerusalem is sacred to both Jews and Muslims because its history is part of their tradition to this day. As I walked down to the Damascus Gate leading into the Old City I thought, 'St

Paul must have trod this road with his letters from the Jewish High Priest entitling him to bring any Christians he found "bound to Jerusalem".' But the narrow gate I passed through had been built by the Ottoman Sultan Suleiman the Magnificent, a Muslim. I entered a maze of crowded alleys flanked on both sides by small shops. Even the shops selling bric-à-brac for Christian tourists all seemed to be owned by Muslims.

Along the stone-paved passages I made my way past women enveloped in black *burqas* buying freshly baked bread which looked like the north Indian naan, oranges from colourful piles of fruit and great hunks of meat carved to their specification by butchers. I resisted the tempting smells from the spiced Arab dishes in the small cafés, and the flat pans full of sweets made on the spot which looked so much more interesting than the mass-produced merchandise on sale in the London I had just come from. I passed a dark stairway guarded by young Israeli soldiers. Their collars were unbuttoned, their shirts hung out untidily over their belts, their berets were stuffed in their pockets and their hair was unkempt. As a young national serviceman in the British Army I had been taught that smartness reflected efficiency and effectiveness. History has shown the Israeli Army to be highly effective, but from what I could see it was certainly not smart. I did pass some Christians – the occasional Greek Orthodox clergyman with his inverted black top hat, Coptic clerics robed in black too, but with flatter headgear, and the long columns of tourists I threaded my way through as I hurried to the church of the Holy Sepulchre. But few of the clergy and none of the pilgrims belonged to the old city.

I wanted to reach the church of the Holy Sepulchre because my guidebook, written by the Roman Catholic Father Jerome Murphy-O'Connor, told me that in spite of scholarly reservation and rival claims this was probably where Jesus was crucified and buried. The exterior of the church was a disappointment, but I had been forewarned by my guidebook which said that 'one expects the central shrine of Christendom to stand out in majestic isolation, but anonymous buildings cling to it like barnacles'. It was impossible to get an idea of the outline of the church from ground level – in fact I had difficulty in even finding it because it was hidden from the passageway by a walled courtyard opposite which stood a mosque. The church was like a shrub striving to survive in an overgrown garden, a symbol of Christianity hemmed in by two faiths that are, at least these days, far more vigorous and combative – Islam and Judaism.

Even here in the heart of the Christian quarter I found myself sitting down to lunch on the pavement outside a Muslim-owned restaurant. Opposite me were Arab shops selling pictures of Jesus. They portrayed the typical European Jesus, often with fair hair and always with a pale skin.

As I ate my houmus and falafel I realized that most Christians were like I was, just visitors to Jerusalem. The only time that Christianity had a political stake in Jerusalem was during the one hundred years in the Middle Ages when it was ruled by the crusaders, a brief and bloody interlude. Although the city is fascinating, it cannot have the impact on Christians that it has on Jews or Muslims. I reflected that perhaps it was not an unfair twist of history that, after Saladin defeated the crusaders, Jerusalem never belonged to the Christians again. In Christianity it is the heavenly Jerusalem that has counted, not the earthly one. The medieval philosopher Peter Abelard wrote his hymn 'Jerusalem the golden, with milk and honey blest' in praise of Heaven. Much more recently Cyril Taylor wrote 'O thou not made with hands', in which 'Jerusalem' is a metaphor for kindly deeds, courage and faith. This tendency to spiritualize real places and events has been part of Christianity from the beginning, and is one of the reasons we have lost touch with the ethnicity of Jesus. We have forgotten his Jewishness. We have forgotten that the land of Israel was precious to him and that he never left it. Instead, we have fashioned him in our own image.

I was brought up to regard Judaism as a strange religion, just as strange as Islam or Hinduism. I was taught that there was only one way to God, and that all who did not follow that road were non-believers, beyond the pale. In fact the Anglican Church into which I was baptized and confirmed seemed to regard the Jews as particularly far outside the pale. In the original Book of Common Prayer the collect or special prayer for Good Friday asks God 'to have mercy on all Jews, Turks, infidels and heretics (a throw-back to the Ottomans, and before them, the Saracens), and take from them all ignorance, hardness of heart and contempt of thy word'. In the 1928 Revised Prayer Book, which was never officially accepted, although it was widely used, the Turks were dropped while the Jews were singled out for special mention, as though they were in particular need of God's grace, further from him than anyone else. On Good Friday God was asked to 'have mercy on thy ancient people the Jews, and upon all who have not known thee'. I am thankful to say that the modern Anglican service for Good Friday contains a much milder prayer to the Lord God of Abraham, which asks him to bless 'the children of your covenant, both Jew and Christian . . . and hasten the coming of your kingdom, when Israel shall be saved, the Gentiles gathered in, and we shall dwell together in mutual love and peace'.

But how many Christians do remember that we are of the same covenant as the Jews, that it was the Jews who first knew the God Jesus believed in, and that they still believe in the same God? It was only when I went to university and started to read about the search for the historical Jesus that it struck me he had been born a Jew, brought up as a Jew and died as a Jew too – not as a Christian.

'O little town of Bethlehem'

In the Holy Land I hoped to discover what Christianity had lost by forgetting the Jewishness of Jesus. But at my first stop outside Jerusalem I was rudely reminded of the minefield I was walking through. The more the history of Jesus is studied, the more historical Jesuses seem to emerge. Scholars seem to disagree about almost everything in the Gospels. How many versions of Jesus would I emerge with when scholars could not even agree whether he was born in Bethlehem, half an hour's bus ride away?

Manger Square in the centre of the town was a shock. Instead of the stillness found by the author of that much loved carol 'O little town of Bethlehem', my ears were assaulted by the noise of tourist buses parked in the square, fouling the atmosphere by running their engines to keep the air conditioning going. In noisy, dusty Bethlehem the Nativity meant making money. Everywhere there were shops selling cheap olive wood and mother of pearl souvenirs of the Christmas scene. But Bethlehem is an Arab town and it is very poor. Tourism is the only chance that most of its people have of making any kind of living. Hurrying past the postcard sellers and the guides offering their

Constantine, the first Christian emperor, and his mother Queen Helena. Constantine's conversion marked the beginning of Christendom, the expression of Christianity through the state as well as through the Church. In the Orthodox Church Constantine and Helena are regarded as saints.

 O̅ Ꙁ ΚΟΝ СΤΗ^ΓΝΟ   ^ΓΝΑ   ЄΛЄΝΙ

services, I stooped to enter the low door leading into the church of the Nativity.

Suddenly I was in a cool, dark, spacious building, flanked with rose-coloured pillars. My guidebook explained that the church is owned jointly by the Greek Orthodox and Armenian Churches. It looks distinctly Eastern with its clusters of icons and dusty candelabra. The present building dates from the sixth century, but it is built on the site of an older church erected on the instructions of the first Christian emperor, Constantine. He had sent his mother, Helena, on an adventure to discover the locations of the Gospel stories. Wherever she went she discovered relics, including, as she thought, the true cross. She decided to build the church of the Nativity over a cave which, local people believed, was the birthplace of Jesus. The Gospels do not mention Jesus being born in a cave, but there is no doubt that Christians have worshipped at this spot from earliest times. In AD 135 the Emperor Hadrian, who wanted to stop the spread of Christianity, had given orders that a shrine to Adonis should be built in the vicinity of the cave. But he achieved the opposite of what he intended, for the existence of the pagan shrine made sure the exact spot was easy for Helena to find when she came looking for it in AD 326.

You can still see the mosaics of the original church underneath the planks that form the modern floor. As I arrived, black-robed priests at the high altar were just completing their worship and in the nave groups of tourists were listening attentively to guides speaking in many different languages. Oil lamps flickered in the small crypt, or cave, beneath the church packed with pilgrims. There was no doubting their devotion as they waited their turn to kneel and kiss the star which marks the place where Jesus is believed to have been born. But was he really born in Bethlehem at all? There is no evidence outside the Bible that he was, and there are many scholars who think the Gospels may not be reliable in saying that he was. The Nativity story only appears in two of the four Gospels, Matthew's and Luke's. Neither John's Gospel nor Mark's Gospel mentions it, and St Paul does not seem to know about it either.

Then there are important differences in what Matthew and Luke have to say about the birth of Jesus. Matthew said that Joseph and Mary had their home in Bethlehem, that Jesus was born there and that they were visited by wise men from the east. Joseph, Mary and the baby Jesus moved to Egypt to escape the wrath of Herod, who had ordered all the children born in and around Bethlehem to be killed. When Herod died the couple moved back to their own country, but went to live in Nazareth and not Bethlehem.

Luke, on the other hand, said that Joseph and Mary lived in Nazareth and came to Bethlehem to register themselves in a census. He dated this as being in the reign of the Emperor Augustus, when a certain Quirinius was the Roman Governor of Syria. Luke also told the story of local shepherds visiting the infant Jesus.

Apart from the inconsistencies between Matthew's and Luke's versions, there are problems with the detail of the stories. There is no record of Herod's massacre of little boys in Bethlehem outside Matthew's Gospel. Nor is there any record of a census that would support Luke's story. There was a census under the Emperor Augustus, but it was in AD 6 not 4 BC, and that was when Quirinius was no longer Governor of Syria. One possibility is that Luke simply got the name of the Governor wrong. Perhaps he did not have access to official records. The Christian writer Tertullian describes a census at the time of Jesus's birth and gives the Governor's name as Saturninus, which has led some scholars to think that he was deliberately correcting Luke.

It looks as though the Gospel writers were trying to fit the stories into the available historical records, but did not always succeed. After Herod's death his kingdom was divided between his sons. Matthew found a reason for Joseph to make his home in Nazareth rather than Bethlehem by saying that he was afraid of Archelaus, who had succeeded Herod in Judaea and Samaria. Joseph would not perhaps have gained much by the move, since in Nazareth he and his family would have been under the rule of another of Herod's sons, Antipas.

Herod and his sons were clients of the Romans, not unlike the Indian Maharajas under the British Raj. The Romans, like the British, retained the power to depose their client kings, as they did with Archelaus in AD 6, when Jesus was still a boy. The Romans took direct responsibility for ruling Archelaus' kingdom, and its capital Jerusalem, with the cooperation of the aristocratic Jewish priests. The priests were left in charge of domestic Jewish affairs.

Coming out of the church, I discussed the question of where Jesus was born with Ed Sanders, an American whom I had invited to guide me on my search for the Jewish Jesus. Ed could well have passed for a businessman. He was in

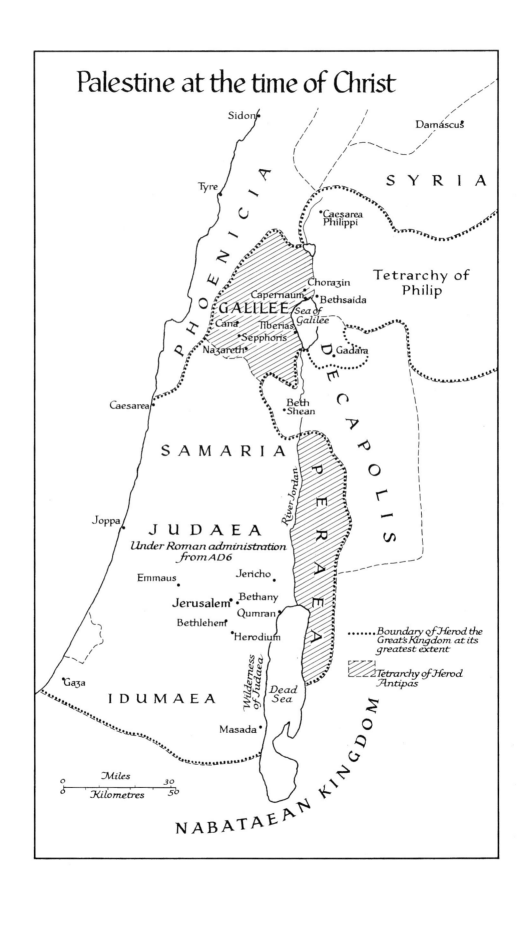

Palestine at the time of Christ

Sidon

Damascus

SYRIA

Tyre

PHOENICIA

Caesarea
Philippi

Tetrarchy of
Philip

Chorazin

Capernaum Bethsaida

GALILEE

Sea of
Galilee

Cana

Tiberias

Sepphoris

DECAPOLIS

Nazareth

Gadara

Beth
Shean

Caesarea

SAMARIA

River Jordan

PERAEA

Joppa

JUDAEA
Under Roman administration
from AD 6

Emmaus

Jericho

Jerusalem

Bethany

Qumran

Bethlehem

Herodium

.... Boundary of Herod the
Great's Kingdom at its
greatest extent

Tetrarchy of Herod
Antipas

Gaza

IDUMAEA

Wilderness
of Judaea

Dead
Sea

Masada

NABATAEAN KINGDOM

Miles
0   30
0   50
Kilometres

his late middle age, a careful dresser, balding, with a well-lived-in face. But he was in fact a distinguished scholar who, after teaching in Canada, had been a professor at Oxford and was now Arts and Sciences Professor of Religion at Duke University in America. He told me that his work was his life. Ed was very insistent that he was a historian, as concerned to discover and relate facts as a scholar who studied any other period of history, not a theologian who might be influenced by faith.

Ed was not convinced that Jesus had been born in Bethlehem, and thought that Matthew and Luke were trying to make the story conform to ancient prophecies. So profoundly did they believe that Jesus was the fulfilment of prophecy that they searched the Hebrew scriptures for all the clues to his divine destiny that they could find. Bethlehem was the town of King David's family. It was where David was anointed by the prophet Samuel to be king over Israel. Many of the Old Testament writings refer to the hope that a descendant of David would one day restore the people to greatness. This would be the Messiah, the Anointed One. The prophet Micah had foretold, 'But you, O Bethlehem Ephrathah, who are little to be among the clans of Judah, from you shall come forth for me one who is to be ruler in Israel, whose origin is from old, from ancient days.' Put all that together and Bethlehem becomes an appropriate birthplace, even the only possible place, for Matthew and Luke to locate the birth of Jesus the Messiah.

Ed didn't believe there was enough hard evidence to say where Jesus was born. He said to me. 'The serious answer is, of course, that I don't know. The only information we have about him is that he came from Nazareth, and that seems to be the simplest assumption – that he was born in Nazareth.' I supposed that might well be so, because people did not move around as much as they do nowadays.

Ed Sanders' view is still challenged by some scholars. Not for the last time on this journey round the Holy Land, I discovered when I turned to the

OVERLEAF
The sixth-century Byzantine nave of
the church of the Nativity in Bethlehem.
Beneath the stone-flagged floor are
the mosaics of the original church, built by
Queen Helena in the fourth century.

guidebook that there was a case to be made for the historical accuracy of the Gospel account. The author of my guidebook, Father Jerome Murphy-O'Connor, is a Dominican, a well-reputed scholar with a depth of learning acquired from his many years in the Holy Land.

Father Jerry accepts Matthew's version that Joseph fled his home when Herod threatened to kill all the children within the Bethlehem area. In support of his argument, history certainly shows that Herod was a very brutal ruler. He executed two out of his ten wives, at least three sons, a brother-in-law and the grandfather of one of his wives. A punitive mass killing to keep the population submissive would have been well within his range. The Roman emperor said he would rather be a pig than Herod's son. Like father, like son could be said of Archelaus, who succeeded Herod in Judaea – though only briefly, for he lacked his father's competence. So, if Matthew is right, Joseph would certainly have had something to fear. Father Jerry is not alone among scholars in believing it to be highly possible that Jesus was born in Bethlehem.

One of the trappings of the Nativity story which have become part of popular Christian piety is clearly not historical – the ox and the ass which surround the Christmas crib. They have their origin, not in the fantasies of Christmas card artists, but in a passage in the first chapter of Isaiah where the prophet is denouncing Israel for failing to know God: 'The ox knows its owner, and the ass its master's crib; but Israel does not know, my people does not understand.' How tempting it must have been to see that reference to the 'master's crib' as a prophecy of the Nativity. The ox and the ass duly appeared as part of the Christmas scene in the early Middle Ages. They don't belong to either Matthew or Luke, or anywhere else in the Bible. But who doesn't associate Christmas with them? What Christmas crib is complete without them?

Of course in one sense Jesus's birthplace is not very important. Wherever he was born, he grew up to be someone so unusual that his followers made extraordinary claims about him – claims which are still made today. But in another sense Bethlehem *is* important. Look through a book of carols and you will see how central Bethlehem is to the Nativity tradition. What Christmas could be complete without singing 'O little town of Bethlehem', or 'While shepherds watched their flocks by night', in which the shepherds are told that Christ was born in 'David's town'.

This for me was the difficulty. Christmas is not just a historical question to be argued over by scholars, it is a myth too. All too often we equate myths with lies, but myths have always been powerful ways of telling great truths. The Greeks did not believe in the literal truth of the myths about their gods, yet those myths underpinned a civilization which we still admire today. They spoke of what I am sure is a most important truth: that man and nature are not distinguishable, that one order underlies or is fundamental to nature and society. If we realized the truth of that conviction we would not be faced with the present environmental crisis.

We live in an era when religious, cultural, philosophical, and now even scientific beliefs are being undermined. In this terrifying confusion, the myth of Christmas still gives faith to millions who would otherwise despair. It gives them faith that there is a God who underpins our world, who really cares for us – perhaps 'loves' would be a better word, if it had not been so debased. It gives them faith that there will be a time when peace will reign. I can understand why scholars want to establish precise facts about the life of Jesus, and why, in doing so, they need to distinguish the facts which can be securely established from myth, legend or speculation. I can also see why it is important for Christianity to accept Jesus as a historical figure: its central claims depend on real people and real events. Yet it would be tragic if the efforts of scholars destroyed the myth. For me, it is still both alive and meaningful. Do we have to make a choice between myth and history? I would rather not, but some seem to think so.

Many believing Christian scholars have tried to resolve this dilemma by separating the myth from the history and so reducing the core of what it is necessary to believe about the life of Jesus. The former Bishop of Durham's views on the Virgin Birth are an example. He is a convinced Christian, sincerely trying to help believers cope with the scepticism of the so-called scientific age, which makes belief in miracles very difficult. But perhaps he has done more harm than good. He had the misfortune to have his views summarized by the media, much of which only reports in headlines, which left many people with the impression that the bishop does not believe in Jesus at all. The baby of Christmas went out with the bathwater, which was not the bishop's intention.

Something good out of Nazareth

I was downcast but not defeated by the controversy over Bethlehem. It seemed to me all the more important to get on to places where we could be more certain about Jesus. I knew there were facts about his life which were almost universally accepted, and reasonable assumptions which could be made. If I tested them against his Jewish background I might find a new conviction that the historical Jesus was a figure substantial enough to carry the meaning of the great myths that underpin the Gospel stories through this age of scepticism and disbelief. Bethlehem, or at least all it stood for, could perhaps survive, whether or not I was certain that Jesus had been born there.

So I went on to Nazareth. There isn't much controversy about this still rather undistinguished town in Galilee. Most authorities agree that Jesus spent his childhood here. The fact that Jesus came from a town which had no great importance in Jewish history embarrassed the early Christians by the time that the Gospels were written. We can catch them trying to deal with their embarrassment in a story from St John's Gospel. Philip, the third Apostle to be called to follow Jesus, told Nathaniel, 'We have found him of whom Moses in the law and also the prophets wrote, Jesus of Nazareth, the son of Joseph.' Nathaniel said to him, 'Can anything good come out of Nazareth?' Philip then answers, 'Come and see.' This incident reflects the scepticism some people felt about Jesus's home town and the way the Church answered it: 'Come and see.' Try spending time in the company of Jesus yourself, and *then* you will know whether anything good can come out of Nazareth.

The early Church's unease about Nazareth is one reason why most scholars agree it must have been Jesus's home. There is a rule of thumb about the Gospels which is widely accepted. Those sayings which do not redound to the credit of Jesus, or do not support the early Church's claims about him, are almost certain to be historically reliable. The Gospels were, after all, written from profound conviction of Jesus's significance. The sceptical would probably describe them as a form of religious propaganda. So when they report something which makes Jesus rather ordinary you can be pretty certain it is true, and only thankful that they did not obscure it altogether. The Gospel writers had nothing to gain by stating that Jesus came from Nazareth. But being stuck with the fact that he did, they find ways of making Nazareth significant.

Luke's Gospel maintains that it was in Nazareth that the Angel Gabriel announced Jesus's impending birth to Mary. This story is of particular importance to many Roman Catholics because it is one of the few Gospel stories in which the mother of Jesus is the central character. There is a vast modern Roman Catholic basilica dedicated to the Annunciation over the cave where Gabriel is believed to have spoken to Mary. The cloisters are an art gallery adorned with mosaics of the Madonna. The Church in Thailand, the Church in Scotland, the Church in America, the Church in India have all sent mosaics. There are madonnas from all corners of the world – well, almost every corner. When I asked the caretaker whether there was a Jewish Mary he replied, 'We gave you the original Madonna, isn't that enough?' He had a point. It made me realize, once again, how the Church has obscured the Jewishness of Jesus.

In the hills of Galilee

From Nazareth I drove towards the Sea of Galilee, passing a long, high ridge known as the Horns of Hattin because of the two sharp peaks at either end. Father Jerry's guidebook told me that this was the ridge where Saladin inflicted his conclusive defeat on the Crusaders, who were fighting under the banner of the King of Jerusalem, Guy De Lusignan. The Crusaders had been without water for more than twenty-four hours and were desperate to reach the spring of Hattin, but a regiment of Saladin's army blocked their way. The vanguard, consisting of the Knights Templar on their heavy horses, charged towards the barrier formed by the Sultan's soldiers. The soldiers wheeled and let the knights gallop past, but then re-formed, blocking the way for the Crusaders' infantry. The Templars rode off, while the infantry broke ranks and ran helter-skelter in search of water. The knights defending the King's tent were unable to withstand Saladin's forces. The Bishop of Acre died clutching a piece of the true cross in his hands. The sacred relic, originally discovered by St Helena, now became a trophy of Saladin's Muslim army.

I was supposed to meet Father Jerry himself at this historic site the next day, but was prevented from doing so by another disaster, this time a natural one

– a bush fire sweeping across the dry grassland. So our meeting took place on another high hill overlooking the Sea of Galilee.

I had memories of the awesome scholarship of Dominicans who used to give an annual series of lectures when I was at university. I was expecting to meet a thin, austere priest clad in white robes, with a complexion pallid from thirty years spent studying in the library of the French Bible School in Jerusalem. Instead, I met a big, burly, florid, man wearing trousers and an open-necked shirt – a jovial priest who had not lost his Irish sense of humour. He told me he had been the first Dominican to break the austere traditions of the Bible School and become a leading figure in the social life of expatriate Jerusalem. He had many friends, he said, among foreign correspondents. But for all his joviality Father Jerry had won a reputation as a scholar, and I soon realized that deep learning underlay his extrovert exterior.

Father Jerry took me back to the controversy about where Jesus was born. He told me that economic history might well support Matthew's statement that Bethlehem, not Nazareth, was Joseph and Mary's original home. He pointed out that when Jesus was a child, Sepphoris, the capital of Galilee, was being rebuilt after being destroyed in 4 BC. Sepphoris was only an hour's walk from Nazareth, and Father Jerry thought that Joseph might have settled there to get work on the reconstruction. He said, 'Nazareth would have served as a base for respectable married men who didn't want their wives and children in a big MacAlpine camp, because you would have had very rough eggs from all over the Roman Empire there.' Father Jerry thought that Joseph was probably more of a small-town general builder than strictly a carpenter – a man who could turn his hand to anything. He believed it was important to understand that Jesus was not brought up in some remote rural backwater. There would have been engineers from Rome, decorators from Italy and artists from Greece working on the rebuilding of Sepphoris. Everyone's second language would have been Greek. That, Father Jerry believes, was reflected in the way Jesus used Greek words such as 'hypocrite'.

So I was not getting the picture I had been brought up with of Jesus being born into a 'meek and lowly' family. His parents were not members of the Jewish élite, but nor were they apparently at the bottom end of the social spectrum either – the outcasts. To rise from that class to become an influential preacher would have been almost miraculous, but it might surely have been quite possible for a man with the cosmopolitan background that Father Jerry suggested. There are some authorities on the New Testament who even say that Joseph might have been a scholar. Aramaic is the language that Jesus almost certainly used, and when the Aramaic word for 'carpenter' is translated in Jewish commentaries on the law, it means a learned man. I would come across a very different view of Jesus's social origins later on, but for now Father Jerry's picture seemed plausible.

Father Jerry and I were sitting high in the Galilean hills. Below us the blue sea glittered in the evening sunlight. Across the sea to the east stood the gaunt brown Golan Heights. To the south, the ugly sprawl of the distant resort town of Tiberias was only a remote scar on the magnificent landscape. We could not see the road which runs along the opposite shore of the sea, nor could we hear the tourist buses roaring along it carrying their pilgrim passengers from sacred site to sacred site. This was Galilee, remote and beautiful. Father Jerry told me how, as a young man, he had been moved by the grandeur of the place. 'When I first saw Galilee it was a marvellous experience. It was in the summer of 1964, and I was on my own in Israel for the first time on a bus from Nazareth, and just as we came over the edge of the hill behind Tiberias I saw the whole lake spread out ahead of me and it was as if the Bible had spoken. The word had come to life in a completely different way, because I could see the places I'd read about. They were real, and somehow history and the concreteness of the presence of God in history were manifest.'

In all the arguments of Bible scholars and historians we can be sure of one thing – Jesus really did walk the hills and the shore of the lake. The sea and the hills, which have changed so little since the first century, bear their own witness to the story of Jesus. They have been described by some as a 'fifth Gospel'. The Galilean countryside is certainly very much part of the four Gospels, and it is clear from them that Jesus was moved by it. His parables are full of metaphors from fishing and farming. It was natural for him to speak of mustard seed, wheat and tares, lilies of the fields, fishing for men and sheep wandering on the hillsides.

OVERLEAF
The Sea of Galilee, the inland sea at the foot of
the Syrian mountains which was the backdrop to
Jesus's ministry. It is less than seven miles from north
to south and about four from east to west.

In contrast Jesus seems to have had little time for the cities. In fact none of the Gospels reports that he taught in Sepphoris, where Joseph might have worked. Nor is Tiberias, which had been built by Herod, ever mentioned in the three synoptic Gospels – Matthew, Mark and Luke, which tend to share the same structure (the Greek-derived 'synoptic' means 'from the same viewpoint'). The cities do not seem to have had much time for Jesus either. Matthew and Luke have Jesus sounding very bitter about his reception in those in which he did teach: 'Woe to you Chorazin! Woe to you Bethsaida! For if the deeds of power done in you had been done in Tyre and Sidon, they would have repented long ago.'

Jesus and John the Baptist

St Mark's Gospel starts with Jesus being baptized by John the Baptist. Apply again the test that the more damaging to the early Church an event in the Gospels is, the more likely it is to have happened, and the baptism of Jesus comes very high on the list of probabilities. In the first place it implies that Jesus regarded himself as a sinner because John was preaching 'a baptism of repentance for the forgiveness of sins'. In the second place, in the Middle Eastern culture of Jesus's time a person of importance would never go to see a lesser person. John should have gone to see Jesus if he had, as the Gospels suggest, known of his divine destiny. The historical likelihood is that Jesus deliberately sought out John for spiritual guidance and accepted baptism at his hands. Most scholars believe that John's statements in the Gospels acknowledging Jesus as his superior were added later to overcome this very difficulty. Even a comparatively orthodox Bible scholar such as Father Jerry is in no doubt that Jesus began his mission as John's disciple. He thinks that Jesus took over the leadership of the movement when John was executed.

John appears to have been what historians call an eschatological prophet. The word 'eschatological' comes from the Greek word for 'last', and so John was a prophet warning of the coming of the last things. There is a warning of divine judgement in the preaching of many of the earlier Hebrew prophets, so John saw himself as the inheritor of a great tradition. He seems to have modelled himself on Elijah, imitating his dress, his preference for living in the wilderness and his fiery preaching style. This would have had a special significance for his contemporaries, because Elijah was due to return to announce the Day of the Lord. But if John saw himself as a latter-day Elijah, that didn't mean, as I was brought up to believe, that he was a prophet of cosmic doom foretelling the end of space, time and the universe. What is more likely is that he believed that some great deliverance was about to take place. There was a lot of speculation in the first century about whether God would intervene to liberate his people from foreign rule. Prophets such as John invoked the precedents of Moses and Joshua to prophesy that God would again save his people from foreign rule. The Jewish historian Josephus wrote scathingly of such people: 'Deceivers and imposters, under the pretence of divine inspiration fostering revolutionary changes, they persuaded the multitude to act like madmen, and led them out into the desert under the belief that God would there give them tokens of deliverance.'

The hope of deliverance was natural, given the fact that the Jews had recently lost their independence again. After revolting against their Syrian rulers the Jews had been governed by the Hasmoneans, a Jewish high priestly family who eventually assumed the title of king. Then in 63 BC the Romans entered Jerusalem after a three-month siege in which twelve thousand Jews were killed. Although the Hasmoneans were by no means always popular rulers, the Jews looked back on their dynasty as a golden age, a time when freedom was snatched from the jaws of tyranny. The Romans did not rule directly but installed the client kings of the Herod family; however, this did nothing to assuage the wound that losing their independence inflicted on Jewish pride. They regarded the kings of the line of Herod as mere quislings of Rome, who had replaced the independent Hasmoneans. Herod and his sons were not even considered proper Jews because they came from Idumaea, to the south of Judaea, which had only recently been converted to Judaism.

So have we now found Jesus's role? If he started as a follower of John, was he too an eschatological prophet, following on where John the Baptist left off, rather like Elisha who succeeded Elijah after his chariot took off for Heaven? Many historians, including Ed Sanders, believe this was how Jesus saw himself. Sanders has written: 'Jesus believed that the promises to Israel would soon be fulfilled; the eschatological restoration of Israel was at hand.'

Inevitably there are other scholars who do not agree. For one thing it is difficult to see how there could be two last prophets, John and Jesus. Father Jerry believes that the Gospels' account is reliable in suggesting that Jesus changed after he started preaching in Galilee. Commenting on Jesus's claim to authority, 'The law said to you but now I say', he explained to me, 'They're not the words of a mere prophet, these are the words of the Messiah. Jesus came to the conviction somehow that he was more than a prophet, that he was the last agent of God in the salvation of the Jews.'

That, of course, is an interpretation which gives Jesus a unique role, that of Messiah, the anointed agent of God in the restoration of Israel. What is difficult to judge from the evidence available is exactly what Jesus thought his role was. At times he seems to be expecting yet another figure to burst in on the scene and bring about God's deliverance, a mysterious 'Son of Man' who comes on the clouds of Heaven. Was this an oblique reference to himself, or did he really think someone else was coming?

Was Jesus a Pharisee?

As I moved on to the pilgrim trail in Galilee I came across a scholar who had marshalled evidence to suggest yet another role for Jesus. He didn't believe that Jesus was unique, but one of many.

I came to Capernaum on the shore of the Sea of Galilee. This, according to the Gospels, was where Jesus made his base during his ministry. It was also the home of Peter, the first and most important of the Apostles. Capernaum plays such an important role in the Gospels that somehow I expected it would still be surviving as a fishing town, but it was as if Jesus's curse had been fulfilled. According to St Matthew's Gospel he had said, 'And you, Capernaum, will you be exalted to Heaven? You shall be brought down to Hades.'

All that has survived of this once prosperous town are a site excavated by archaeologists; a partially restored synagogue; a small Roman Catholic monastery; a Roman Catholic church, built over what Franciscan archaeologists believe are the remains of Peter's house; and a charming Greek Orthodox church with strawberry-coloured domes. The modern Catholic

The Baptism of Christ in a fifteenth-century
Italian landscape. The dove that hovers above Jesus is
a symbol of the Holy Spirit, which descends on
Jesus, confirming his identity as the Son of God.
Painting by Piero della Francesca, 1450s.

church could certainly not be called charming. To me it resembled nothing so much as the superstructure of an underground car park. The two churches symbolize the rivalry between Roman Catholic and Orthodox Christians for control of the sacred sites. The synagogue was built much later than the time of Jesus, but may stand on the site of the synagogue where, according to the synoptic Gospels, he taught, healed and got into trouble with the Pharisees. Appropriately enough a rabbi, David Rosen, had come to meet me at this site.

Rosen, with his jet-black hair and beard, seemed young to have held the important post of Chief Rabbi, both in Ireland and in Cape Town, South Africa. He was now teaching at the Jerusalem Centre for Near Eastern Studies. He talked fast, clearly and without a trace of uncertainty.

When I asked him how he saw Jesus, he shot back. 'He was a Jewish rabbi. He was born as a Jew, taught as a Jew, preached as a Jew and died as a Jew.'

'Wait a minute', I thought. 'That would make Jesus a Pharisee, and surely they were his arch-enemies?'

When I asked David Rosen whether he was saying that Jesus was a Pharisee he replied, 'The whole of his teaching is rooted within what we call Pharisaic Judaism, Rabbinic Judaism, the world out of which Judaism of today emerged. There's hardly a word of Jesus that is not to be found in a parallel saying by the rabbis.'

'But we were taught to believe that the Pharisees were sticklers for the Law, while Jesus was all about love.'

'I would point out,' replied Rosen, 'that the concept of the "love of God" appears many more times in the Hebrew Bible and Pharisaic literature than the concept of the fear of God.'

I still have with me the Cruden's Concordance which I bought as a theology student to enable me to find the different places where particular words were mentioned in the Bible. I looked up the word 'Pharisee' and found this description: 'Jesus denounced the Pharisees for their hypocrisy, which was shown by their care for the minutest formalities imposed by the traditions of the elders, not for the mind and heart which should correspond. They were ambitious, arrogant and proudly self-righteous, all of which qualities were contrary to the teachings of Jesus.' Now here was David Rosen saying we should scrub the word 'Pharisaical' from the dictionary. They were not hypocrites, apparently, but were as concerned with love as Jesus was. So how had this massive misunderstanding arisen?

Rosen explained that it was the result of the Jewish Christians breaking away from what he called 'the Jewish national context'. It was an interpretation designed to show 'the superiority of one as against the other'. Rosen did not rule out the possibility of Jesus having disputes with some Pharisees. He said, 'In the Talmud – the commentaries on the Law – there is a description of seven kinds of Pharisees, which shows the diversity amongst them themselves. Sometimes the commentators are quite belittling to certain elements that call themselves Pharisees. For example, one Pharisaic rabbi speaks of the sages, his contemporaries, and he says, "Beware of them because their bite is a bite of a fox, their hiss is the hiss of a viper, and their sting is the sting of a scorpion." Well, this is the kind of language of internal debate.' As he said this I was reminded that Christians, too, used strong, argumentative language as the divisions between them developed.

What David Rosen made me realize was that the Judaism of Jesus's time must have been very different from the Judaism of today. Almost all Jewish life nowadays comes from rabbinic Judaism. As Rosen had said, the Pharisees were the forerunners of the rabbis. But in Jesus's day they were only one group of Jews. There were also the Sadducees, the priestly aristocrats who were the dominant party in the running of the temple, and the strict Essenes, who were extremely punctilious in their observation of the Law. I would find out more about the Essenes when I got to Qumran.

We know about these three groups or sects of Judaism because they are described in the writings of the Jewish historian Josephus, a near contemporary of Jesus. The Pharisees were apparently more liberal than the Essenes. They wanted to help ordinary people observe their faith in daily life not by extreme practices but by regular prayer, careful observation of the laws of purity, and acts of charity. The religion of the Sadducees was based on a literal reading of the scriptures and on the temple with its round of sacrifices. The Pharisees taught that sacrifice was first and foremost a spiritual duty. Alongside the Pharisees, Essenes and Sadducees were intellectuals who read Greek philosophy and tried to reconcile it with Jewish belief, and a range of charismatic healers and teachers who would have had a personal following, particularly among the poor. So the Pharisees were not, as I had been taught to believe, narrow-minded, legalistic bigots, but the most liberal of the major Jewish sects in the time of Jesus. I could see the attractiveness of the theory that Jesus was one of them.

There are non-Jewish scholars, too, who recognize that Jesus has a good deal in common with the Pharisees. Ed Sanders, for instance, has written, 'There are few sign points of tension between Jesus and the Jewish leaders of his time.' Sanders has also pointed out that if Jesus had preached against the Jewish Law, saying it was wrong, there would have been very serious consequences because he would in effect have been saying that Moses and God got it wrong. There were, of course, serious consequences: Jesus was crucified. But as we shall see, that was probably not because he preached against the Jewish Law or quarrelled with the Pharisees.

But David Rosen does not believe that Jesus was just another Pharisee. He said to me, 'I think his teachings are of enormous richness within the context of traditional Jewish teaching, and it's a great tragedy that, due to the terrible polemic against Jews and the violence and prejudice acted on throughout the ages, the beauty in Jesus's teaching is not known to most of the Jewish community.'

The miracle worker

One of my mentors as I prepared my search for the Jewish Jesus was Geza Vermes, another Jewish scholar who had once been a Catholic priest. He recognizes a unique power in Jesus's teaching and has written, 'In Jesus's ethical code there is a sublimity, distinctiveness, and originality in form unparalleled in any other Hebrew code; neither is there any parallel to the remarkable art of his parables.' But Vermes does not believe that Jesus was a Pharisee. He finds another role for him within the society of his day as an exorcist, healer and teacher – a holy miracle worker. Vermes writes about a strange character called Honi the Circle Drawer, a legendary Jewish saint of the first century. Like Jesus, he seems to have had an intensely intimate relationship with God. He also irritated his fellow Jews, who thought he was impertinent in his approach to the Almighty. But what Honi was best known for was his ability to make rain. When he prayed for a drought to end, it did. Vermes believes that Jesus may have been regarded as a holy man rather like Honi.

My next stop in Galilee was to bring me face to face with the problem of Jesus the miracle worker. It was the Benedictine church of the Multiplication of the Loaves and Fishes, the place on the shore of the Sea of Galilee where pilgrims are told that Jesus fed the multitude. Inside the church I listened to an American preacher telling a group of pilgrims the meaning of this story. 'The miracle,' he said, 'teaches us that whatever our needs Jesus will provide if we pray to him.' I didn't find this very helpful. Surely one of the problems of believers is that so often their prayers are not answered, or at least not answered in the way they expect them to be. Besides which, were the pilgrims really required to believe that Jesus could perform the miracle of feeding five thousand people with five loaves and a two small fishes and that twelve basketfuls were left over? This seemed very much the Jesus of the Church, not the Jesus of his own time, the Jewish Jesus.

St John's Gospel tells us that the first miracle was the replenishing of the wine at the marriage in Cana of Galilee. It is a miracle which I like very much, because it shows that the early Church did not think of Jesus as the narrow-minded moralist, the puritan who was against all enjoyment that I had heard about from so many pulpits. Later in the same chapter St John's Gospel says, 'Many believed in his name when they saw the miracles which he did.' But in the scientific era in which we live Jesus's miracles are a source of disbelief. 'How can you believe in the Gospels with all those miracles which couldn't possibly have happened?' is a question often asked of Christians. Yet they were not apparently a stumbling-block to those pilgrims in the Benedictine church.

It is possible that some of the miracle stories were based on rumours. As a journalist I know the power of rumours today in spite of all our sophisticated methods of communication. Rumours would have abounded in a society where most information was carried by word of mouth. And rumours very soon become facts, because it is what people believe happened, not what actually happened, which counts, and which gets passed down from generation to generation. The Gospel writers would have been inclined to believe the miracles because they appeared to confirm Old Testament prophecies, and to depict Jesus as the successor of the Old Testament heroes. The feeding miracles, for instance, have echoes of the story of God coming to the help of Moses when his querulous followers complained that they would rather have been killed in Egypt than come into the wilderness to die of starvation. God sent quails in the evening, and in the morning the dew turned into bread.

There are, however, those who believe that the spectacular miracles – the two feeding stories, the calming of the storm, the walking on water and others which are not healings – could perfectly well have happened. They argue that modern science does show that we do not live in such a regulated, or perhaps I should say regimented, world as we once thought. Nature is not as predictable as Newton led us to believe. There may be powers within nature which we do not yet know about, powers which can be released by prayer and faith. This leaves room for the possibility of a God who is constantly involved in the world, who does act in ways that we might call irregular, just as nature sometimes acts unpredictably. I think most people who are not total sceptics would want to keep their options open on whether miracles happen. It was Ed Sanders who said to me, 'I don't think that fish multiply just by being broken apart, but I don't think that the early Christians were a lot of liars, frauds and cheats, either. So I don't know how to explain these nature miracles. I'm at a loss. I have to admit it.' Another American Bible scholar and theologian, Marcus Borg, has said that these miracles will have to be put in a 'historical suspense account'.

Borg has put forward solid reasons for believing that Jesus did perform what were seen as healing miracles. In the first place, they are widely attested. Secondly, healings and exorcisms did occur frequently in those days. And thirdly, even Jesus's opponents admitted that he performed miracles, accusing him of being in league with the devil. As Borg put it, 'By admiring followers and sceptical foes alike he was seen as a holy man with healing powers.' Nowadays we are told that there are medical and psychological explanations for miracles, but many people still believe they occur. In Jesus's time people lived in the conviction that there was more going on in the world than meets the eye. There was a world of spirit interacting with everyday life. It was, as Borg has said, 'not simply an article of belief but an element of faith'. So there is no reason to doubt that in his time Jesus did heal people and that the cures were accepted as miraculous. They are important historically because they suggest that Jesus might have been what Borg has called 'a spirit-filled person in the charismatic stream of Judaism'. That would be a somewhat different role from David Rosen's Pharisee, or Ed Sanders' eschatological prophet.

I walked from the church of the Multiplication of the Loaves and fishes to the next sacred site just up the road. Here the Roman Catholic Church really had implanted its version of Jesus on Galilee. There was a chapel dedicated to the Primacy of Peter. Standing in the garden a small black South African Franciscan, Father Thomas, directed pilgrims inside, politely insisting on proper dress – no shorts – and checking his schedule to make sure that the right group held a service at the open-air altar at the right time. He smiled so much that he reminded me of the famous Anglican South African Archbishop, Desmond Tutu.

I said to Father Thomas, 'So this is where Jesus told Peter he was the rock on which he would build the Church.' But my knowledge of the Gospels had failed me.

The Franciscan smiled and said, 'So many pilgrims come here thinking that, but that actually happened in Caesarea Philippi, on the sea coast, not on the coast of this lake.'

'So what happened here?'

'The church is built over the rock on which Jesus is said to have had breakfast after the Resurrection, not the rock on which he built his Church.'

'And what then has St Peter to do with it?'

'This was the time when Jesus told Peter to feed his sheep, and that's what Peter's successor, the Pope, still does.' He roared with laughter and I joined in.

Inside the chapel I found the rock in front of the altar. Outside, I paddled with other pilgrims in the water lapping over what appeared to be the ruins of an earlier building. According to Father Jerry's guidebook, the heart-shaped stones were known as the twelve thrones and were probably taken from a disused building to commemorate the twelve Apostles.

This was a charming place – a place which clearly inspired great devotion in the pilgrims hearing mass at the altar in the garden, but not perhaps a place marking a historical incident. The breakfast only appeared in St John's Gospel. After the Resurrection Peter and his colleagues had returned to Galilee and their original occupation. At the end of an unsuccessful night's fishing they saw a stranger standing on the shore who told them where to cast their nets. The catch was miraculous, and one of the disciples recognized the stranger as Jesus. After breakfasting on some of the fish Jesus renewed his original call to Peter, even though he had betrayed him. St John's Gospel is acknowledged by all scholars to be the least historical, and the details of the post-Resurrection stories are generally considered to be questionable. Yet the Roman Catholic Church revered this site. Could that be, I wondered, because

the commission to Peter, 'Feed my sheep', supported its claim that the Pope, as the Apostle's successor, was the Supreme Pontiff of the universal Church? That suspicion, I realized, did not necessarily mean that Jesus had not appeared to the disciples here, but it did remind me how many layers of Christian history had to be peeled away to get to the Jewish Jesus, and how firmly Christians had claimed Galilee for their own.

I left Galilee stunned by the beauty of the blue water and the hills surrounding it, convinced that Jesus must have been deeply moved by this beauty too, but worried that Christians seemed to be more interested in the not very distinguished churches they had erected. I had felt the presence of God in the remoteness of the hills, not in the churches. Galilee had strengthened my conviction that Christianity has got far too removed from nature, that the Church needed to be reminded what the beauty of Galilee must have meant to Jesus. I may be a romantic, but I am glad that not all Christians have been insensitive to the beauty of Galilee, because one of the most popular hymns, 'Dear Lord and Father of mankind', contains the verse,

O Sabbath rest by Galilee,
O calm of hills above,
Where Jesus knelt to share with thee,
The silence of eternity,
Interpreted by love.

The Message of the Dead Sea Scrolls

Had Galilee given me a clearer picture of the historical Jesus? Well, in one strange way, yes. Just walking along the shore he must have walked, and climbing the hills he must have climbed, brought home to me that Jesus was a historical figure, that he did once exist. While questioning, and all too often losing faith in the Jesus that the Church had taught me to believe in, I had, I realized, subconsciously come to doubt his very existence. There are, I am

The Dead Sea Scrolls are thought to
be the library of a community
of the Essenes, an ascetic Jewish sect
at the time of Jesus.

sure, millions of people in countries with a Christian tradition who are not aware of the fact that Jesus is as historical a figure as their own kings and queens whom they are taught about at school. One reason so many people do not think that Jesus really existed is because they have got the impression that the Church made it all up. That impression has been strengthened by some of the speculation that has followed the discovery of the Dead Sea Scrolls.

The scrolls have made Qumran, on the shores of the Dead Sea, a major tourist attraction. There I saw narrow slits in the rock of a hillside, entrances to the cave where the scrolls were discovered. They were found by pure chance when, in 1947, a Bedouin shepherd boy threw a stone into one of the caves and heard the sound of something shattering. He went in to investigate and found he had broken a pot containing manuscripts. That was the beginning of the long-running story of the Dead Sea Scrolls discrediting the Gospels. It still runs, because there are journalists who claim to have evidence that the Roman Catholic Church is sitting on some of the scrolls which are particularly damaging to its version of the life and times of Jesus. In fact, the reason for suspicion about the scrolls is very mundane – scholarly infighting. So important was the find that scholars hoarded the texts, refusing to hurry the task of translation or to share the originals with others. Years of scholarly silence encouraged the rumour that there was a terrible secret being kept from the public.

Although it was quite early in the morning when I met the Jewish historian Zwi Werblowsky at Qumran, it was already uncomfortably hot. An elderly man, as jovial as Father Jerry, he was delighted when I asked him about the theory that the Vatican was sitting on some of the scrolls because they disproved the Church's Jesus.

'Yes, I'm very fond of these theories,' said the professor, grinning, 'because I'm always fond of fools who are, as the Americans say, hung up on conspiracy theories. The more something appears to be shocking the more it hits the headlines.' He went on to explain, 'The importance of the sect for a better understanding of the message and ministry of Jesus is that it highlights the difference between them.'

The Essenes were the sect whose rituals and rules of life are described in the Dead Sea Scrolls. They are one of the three Jewish sects described by Josephus, but unlike the other two – the Pharisees and the Sadducees – they find no mention in the Gospels. The Jewish scholar Geza Vermes has described the Essenes as 'fanatical' in their observance of the Mosaic Law. Since one of the Gospel writers' main themes was that Jesus put love above the Law, I wondered why they did not report conflicts with the Essenes as well as with the Scribes and Pharisees. Professor Werblowsky told me he thought the Essenes might have been left out because they had ceased to exist by the time the Gospels were written. That would certainly fit in with Rabbi David Rosen's belief that much of the polemic against the Pharisees in the Gospels was not true of the time of Jesus but was a later addition which sprang from the hostility between them and the early Christians. If there were no Essenes by then, they could not have been the focus of early Christian hostility.

The Dead Sea Scrolls reveal that the Essenes lived a way of life very different from that of Jesus. There were, apparently, two different Essene rules. Those who subscribed to the Community Rule lived together under strict discipline. Most scholars believe Qumran was a kind of monastery, and its members were probably celibate for long periods of time. Those who obeyed what was known as the Damascus Rule lived in the world, but remained apart from their Jewish and Gentile neighbours. Jesus certainly did not live in a monastery and wherever he went he mixed with people – he 'ate and drank with tax collectors and sinners'. So we have a contrast between the rigidly conservative Essenes and the revolutionary Christians. We have the Essenes of both rules keeping themselves to themselves, and Jesus eating with anyone who came along. The Essenes were ascetics, whereas all the Gospel evidence goes to suggest that Jesus was not. He was reported to have been accused of gluttony and drunkenness by his detractors. They would have chosen different allegations to make against him if he had been an ascetic preaching asceticism. It does not seem very likely that the Vatican would want to hide evidence of the differences between Jesus and one of the major Jewish sects of his time. You would think such differences would actually support a case for the 'specialness' of Jesus. Although Christians still believe that Jesus fulfilled the Jewish Bible's prophecies, they have since the days of the earliest Church wanted to distinguish, even separate, Jesus from his Jewish background. I realized that the importance of the Dead Sea Scrolls in my search for the Jewish Jesus was that they ruled out one option – he was not an Essene.

But what else could we learn from the Scrolls? I asked professor Werblowsky.

He replied, 'You can understand Jesus and John the Baptist much better if you see them in opposition to the Essenes. Just as you can understand Luther and the Reformation much better if you see them against the Catholic background of the sixteenth century.'

So it appeared that, seen against the background of first-century Jewish society, Jesus might have been a Pharisee, a miracle-working holy man, or a prophet warning that God was about to intervene in human affairs. But that of course did not answer what for me was the most important question – could he also have been the Jesus of the early Church, the Christian Jesus? That Jesus was more than a particularly gifted teacher, or an unusually charismatic miracle worker, or a prophet in the line of the great Old Testament prophets. To answer that question I had to move on to the scene of the drama of the end of Jesus's life – the holy city of Jerusalem.

Who killed Jesus?

Driving back into Jerusalem, I caught sight of the tower of what looked like an English parish church to the east of the Old City. It was, I was told, the Anglican Cathedral, appropriately enough dedicated to St George. I decided to go there the following Sunday for the eight o'clock service of Holy Communion. Listening to the familiar words, I realized that the whole service was based on the events of the last few days of Jesus's life – the Last Supper, his death on the cross and his Resurrection. It was because of the way the Church remembered these events that the historical Jewish Jesus had been transformed into the divine Christ of Christian faith.

The crucifixion seemed to be the key to it all, the central point of the Christian faith. It was a historical fact that was not doubted by any of the scholars I had met or in any of the books I had read. The only community who doubted it were the Muslims, who believe that it was not the real Jesus who was crucified, but a substitute. It occurred to me that, if I could get an inkling into Jesus's intentions, it might help. Did he deliberately court arrest and brutal execution, or did he not appreciate how dangerous it was to provoke the authorities. Was it an accident? If Jesus intended to be killed, what purpose did he think that would serve? Who did Jesus believe he was when he was nailed to the cross?

Not only did I need to find out what Jesus's intentions were, I had to discover who was responsible for his death. The two questions went together. A great deal of confusion has been created in the minds of Christians because preachers have tended to lump all the Jewish religious teachers together as enemies of Jesus. The Gospels themselves are far from clear or consistent about who his enemies were. For instance, in St Mark's Gospel, when Jesus heals a man with a withered hand on the Sabbath it is the Pharisees and the Herodians who discuss how they might destroy him. St Matthew's Gospel, apparently reporting the same incident, has only the Pharisees opposing Jesus, but according to St Luke the Scribes and the Pharisees were after him. In other passages Matthew has the Sadducees coming to tempt Jesus. Luke seems to be obsessed by lawyers who ask Jesus trick questions, while John's Gospel simply talks about 'the Jews'. David Rosen seemed to think that Jesus may have been a Pharisee and that the polemic against the Pharisees was added to the story of Jesus years after his death, when the other groups had died out and only the Pharisees were left. So who really wanted to get Jesus killed?

The last days of Jesus

Jesus came to Jerusalem on his fateful last journey ostensibly to celebrate Passover, along with tens of thousands of Jews not only from Palestine but from Asia Minor, North Africa, and the cities of the Mediterranean. Three of the four Gospels describe how Jesus had arranged an upper room to be prepared where he could eat the Passover meal with the disciples. It was after this meal that Jesus took his closest companions to the Garden of Gethsemane in the Kidron Valley where he was arrested.

I went first with Father Jerry to the Kidron Valley. At the time of Jesus it was outside the city boundaries, but now it is part of Jerusalem. We sat on one side of the valley looking across at the garden of Gethsemane and the Mount of Olives. A busy main road bisected the hillside. 'Couldn't the motor car leave this revered place alone?' I wondered. 'After all, it's the Jews' most sacred burial ground, the place where they believe the Final Judgement will take place, as well as the site of the agony of Jesus.' I could see a crowd of Orthodox Jews in wide-brimmed hats and tailcoats standing around a grave which had just been dug in the hillside.

Father Jerry, this time wearing the white robes of a Dominican, told me what he believed happened on that last night. Pointing to a large tomb with a top like a bottle, he said, 'You see the Pharaoh's bonnet? There are three other tombs that are visible that would have been there in Jesus's time. Remember it was full moon, it was Passover. It must have been a very eerie place on that night,' he added.

I asked Father Jerry why Jesus prayed for the cup to be taken away – whether he knew he was going to die.

'It suddenly hit Jesus that it might be tonight,' he said. 'It was a moment of panic. The language that's used is very strong. He's breaking down physically through fear. The personality is disintegrating. Then he collapses on the ground, and he said, "If it's possible, take this cup away from me." It doesn't sound much like a prayer to me. "If it's possible" – he's not even sure that God can help him.'

'So he's lost God at that stage?' I asked.

'Yes. This is to me a cry of despair, which doesn't last very long. It's a very human emotion. He pulls himself together and then says to his disciples, "Let us be going."'

'But you believe very strongly in the humanity of Jesus. Isn't it possible that he said, "Let's be going, let's get away quickly, get out of here."?'

'That's entirely possible, because he did that several times in Galilee. Here he had exactly the same option – remember, it was the Jews who were after him and they had no army. All he had to do was keep ahead of them. Fifteen minutes to the top of the Mount of Olives, twenty minutes to Bethany, then into the desert where no one would find him. He would have been perfectly safe.'

'And what do you believe? Do you believe he thought of escaping, or that he waited there deliberately so that he could be arrested?'

'I think that on this occasion Jesus thought it was inappropriate to take a walk up the hill. I think he had come to the realization that his death would be not the abortion of his ministry, the death of his ministry, but the means whereby his ministry would be fulfilled – that it would be a saving event.'

Father Jerry could see the whole story of the Passion fitting into the landscape we saw before us, but I knew I had to be cautious. The whole account of Jesus's prayer, arrest and trial was written by Christians who were totally convinced that he was the divine Son of God who was going to a death that had already been planned for the salvation of the world. Behind that Passion narrative lay the sombre words of Old Testament prophecy. Was the story of Jesus's death deliberately written in such a way that it would show he fulfilled those prophecies? There is, for instance, the fifty-third chapter of the Book of Isaiah:

> He was despised and rejected by men; a man of sorrows, and acquainted with grief; and as one from whom men hide their faces he was despised, and we esteemed him not.
>
> Surely he has borne our griefs, and carried our sorrows; yet we esteemed him stricken, smitten of God, and afflicted. But he was wounded for our transgressions, he was bruised for our iniquities; upon him was the chastisement that made us whole, and with his stripes we are healed.

Those words were written five hundred years before the time of Jesus when the Jews were in exile in Babylon. The prophet who wrote them was probably trying to console his people by showing them that the sufferings of Israel were not in vain. But from our point of view they certainly seem to echo the Passion story, and it is no surprise that the Church has traditionally interpreted them as foretelling the Crucifixion. By writing the Passion story as though it was a fulfilment of Isaiah's prophecy the Gospel writers reassured the first Christians that Jesus's death was part of the divine plan.

There are also scholars who, unlike Father Jerry, do not believe that Jesus went to Jerusalem on that Passover knowing he was destined to die. Marcus Borg, for instance, has written, 'The outcome was not the purpose of the journey.' According to Borg, Jesus went to Jerusalem at the time of year when it would contain the largest gathering of Jews in order to issue a call for change.

When I asked Ed Sanders what Jesus intended he was, as usual, cautious. 'This is one of the harder questions. Did he know in advance that he was going to take actions and say things that would put his life in jeopardy? I'm not sure he would have. He himself may have seen this Passover in advance as being the time when he was going to make his boldest statement.' Geza Vermes believes that the death of Jesus was an unfortunate accident. He sees Jesus as

A reconstruction of Herod's Temple, the pride of Jerusalem in the time of Jesus. One of the reasons for the opposition Jesus found in Jerusalem was that he prophesied the destruction of this mighty edifice.

a holy man from the countryside, out of his depth in the big, crowded city. He made some kind of miscalculation in what he said and did, which led to his arrest and death. He was simply in the wrong place at the wrong time.

What was it that Jesus said and did that led to his death? Most scholars agree that the incidents in the Temple are the most likely explanation for the Crucifixion. The action which Jesus took in the Temple in Jerusalem, and the words he spoke there, might therefore give some clue as to his intentions. He must have known that 'driving out those who sold and those who bought' was a highly provocative action, and that prophesying the Temple's destruction would enrage the priests. Did he lose his temper? Were his words symbolic prophecies? Or did he deliberately pick a fight with the Temple authorities knowing that it might lead to his execution?

The Temple: focus of Jewish faith

Although the Jews have never built another Temple to replace Herod's, the concept still has a very deep meaning for many of them. All that remains of that Temple is the wall which supported its esplanade and part of the lintel of a gate. Temple Mount is crowned not by a Jewish shrine but by the magnificent gold-domed mosque built at the end of the seventh century which dominates the landscape of Jerusalem. But when I went to the square below Temple Mount it was packed with joyful Jewish families, clapping, and what sounded to me like yodelling as they celebrated barmitzvahs to mark the coming to manhood of their sons. Black-suited Orthodox Jews with black hats and long curled sideboards, known as Chazam, moved among the crowd offering to help with the ceremonies or organize groups of ten to pray together. Some preferred to pray alone, swaying back and forwards as if in a trance in front of what has come to be known as the Wailing Wall. Others touched the wall with reverence and then kissed their hands. This was the most sacred place in the world for them to pray – so sacred that Jews who cannot get to Jerusalem fax their prayers to the post office in Jaffa Road from where they are taken and stuffed into the cracks between the massive stones of the wall. My guide also told me that rebuilding the Temple was part of the hope of the restoration of Israel.

In Jesus's time the Temple was the centre of the Jewish faith, and every Jew was encouraged to worship there three times a year, one of which was the feast of the Passover. Temples in general were a familiar sight in the ancient world. Every city had its favourite gods and supported priests who offered sacrifices and tended the divine images. But the Jews only had one Temple to one God. If you did not live in Jerusalem it was too bad – you either had to travel there to worship at the Temple or do without. It was quite a distance to travel from Galilee to Jerusalem, as Jesus did; if you lived, as many Jews did, in Egypt or Syria, you could only afford to go every so often. Although those Jews who faced difficulties in getting to the Temple regularly found other ways of worshipping, it still retained its symbolic importance for them.

The Temple was the one place where God was present with his people. Its central point was the sanctum sanctorum, or holy of holies, which consisted of two rooms. In the first room there was an altar and a table for what was known as the shewbread, which only the priests were allowed to eat. The second room was empty, and it was so sacred that no one was allowed to enter it except the high priest – and even he only entered on the Day of Atonement to sprinkle blood in expiation of sin. In pagan temples it was this back room which housed the image of the god. The presence of the Jewish God, though, could not be in the form of an image because images were strictly forbidden. Instead the presence was indicated by an empty space. Non-Jews found this extraordinary. The Roman general Pompey scandalized the Jews when he entered the holy of holies in the Jerusalem Temple in AD 63. He seems to have been curious to discover whether there really was anything inside. There were rumours that the Jews secretly housed a terrifying or obscene image. Some people even thought they worshipped a pig! But Pompey reported, rather disappointedly, that the inner shrine really was empty.

It was in the outer courts that animals were sacrificed. The slaughter of sheep at Passover was particularly dramatic. Ed Sanders estimated that thirty thousand would have been killed in a matter of hours, with the result that 'the courts would have been awash with blood', as he put it.

In Jesus's time the Temple was not just a place of worship and sacrifice. It was also the power base of the priests who controlled Jerusalem, and the tithes that every Jew was supposed to pay supported them and their administration. The Temple was both a central bank and a kind of law court, and it was run by the high priest with the backing of a council. Many members of the council would have been Sadducees, but there were probably some

A sculpture on the victory Arch of Titus in Rome depicts the humiliation
the Romans brought on the Jews by destroying the Jerusalem
Temple in AD 70. The seven-branched candlestick, the table of
the shewbread and the sacred trumpets are carried off as booty.

high-class Pharisees too. The 'scribes' and 'lawyers' mentioned in the gospels were just the kind of people who would have been members of the Council: highly educated experts in law, ritual, tradition and economics.

Like many other places of worship the Temple was very wealthy, and made a lot of money for those who controlled it too. In Jerusalem I met a scholar who described to me the extortionate demands made on pilgrims in the Temple. Professor Yak'hov Meshorer, one of Israel's leading archaeologists, was an elderly man, soft spoken and with a gentle sense of humour. He took me to one of the graves in the Valley of Kidron to demonstrate how wealthy the rich Jews of Jerusalem were. It was a cave hacked out of hard limestone. Only the very richest families, Professor Meshorer explained, could have afforded to pay for the land, the work involved in excavating the burial chamber, and the decoration of this grave which was large enough to house the dead of many generations. He told me of the Hail family, the family of a priest. They had become extremely wealthy from collecting taxes, gifts and other money in the Temple. He showed me a silver shekel which was the only coinage accepted for payment of the Temple taxes.

When I suggested that it might be one of the coins which fell to the ground when Jesus upset the tables of the money changers he replied, 'It could be, yes, although there are seven thousand of them known today.'

'Why,' I asked, 'did Jesus overturn the money changers' tables?'

'I think he resented the fact that the Temple authorities created laws that forced the Jews to pay more than they actually had to. To buy these shekels from the money changers and pay it back as tribute they had to add eight per cent, which is really too much for changing money.' Professor Meshorer also told me that Jews had to pay well over the top for the holy pigeons reared by the priests which were sacrificed in the Temple. That was why, he believed, Jesus threw the pigeon sellers out of the Temple. We know that the Essenes, too, were dissatisfied with the Temple: they thought it was totally corrupt.

So it is possible that Jesus was enraged by the corruption he saw in the Temple and lost his temper, which was why he caused such a commotion there. If we accept David Rosen's theory that Jesus was a Pharisee it is possible that his actions may in some way have been connected with the long-running hostility between the Pharisees and the Sadducees who dominated the management of the Temple. In the first century BC the high priest and governor of Jerusalem sided with the Sadducees in a dispute and eight hundred Pharisees were crucified. So if Jesus was a Pharisee that would make it even more likely that his intention was to demonstrate against the way the Temple was being run. With my Christian upbringing I automatically think of Jesus's Jewish enemies as the Scribes and Pharisees, but most scholars appear to think that the high priest and his colleagues were his enemies in the last week in Jerusalem.

According to the Gospels, Jesus did more than demonstrate his anger against the corrupt practices in the Temple. He prophesied that it would be destroyed. Ed Sanders is not convinced that Jesus ever accused the Temple authorities of turning the place into a den of robbers, but he does believe that Jesus threatened the Temple. If Jesus was, as Ed thinks, an eschatalogical prophet, then his actions in the Temple were symbolic. Jesus meant that God himself would destroy the Temple as a prelude to bringing about a new and perfect order.

If Jesus did prophesy the destruction of the Temple, this can be taken quite literally as a prophecy fulfilled. In the years after Jesus's death there was a violent revolt by the Jews against Roman rule, and the whole nation rose up in a last desperate struggle for independence. The Romans had been patient with Jewish resentment, but this time they were brutal. In AD 70 Roman armies marched into Jerusalem and burnt the Temple to the ground. The treasures of gold, the bronze vessels and the glittering candelabra were carried off to Rome as booty. The Temple was never rebuilt.

Sitting on the steps below Temple Mount, Ed Sanders interpreted Jesus's prophecy rather differently. 'It pans out some forty or so years after Jesus's death,' he said, 'but the destruction Jesus looked for was one that was part and parcel of God bringing a new and better age, and I think that the conquest of Judea by the Roman army would not have looked to him like the fulfilment of the arrival of the kingdom.'

'What did Jesus imagine God's intervention would be?' I asked Ed.

'In the words of the Lord's prayer, Jesus hoped that the time could come when God's will was done on Earth as in Heaven. The kingdom of God for Jesus and for other Jews who hoped for it did not mean the destruction of the world. It meant its reordering. God would step in and directly change the world so that would be a better place. I think that is what Jesus longed for.'

'What was Jesus's role to be in this better world?'

'Jesus seems to have thought that his disciples would judge the twelve tribes of Israel. St Matthew says, "In the new world, when the Son of Man shall sit on his glorious throne, you who have followed me will also sit on twelve thrones, judging the twelve tribes of Israel." If his disciples were to judge the twelve tribes, surely Jesus was above the disciples? That makes him, I think, in his own estimation the viceroy – that is, God is King and Jesus will govern in his place in this new and better age.'

Although some modern scholars regard Jesus's sayings about the kingdom to come as later interpolations by the Gospel writers, no one can deny that the early Church did expect Jesus to return. St Paul pictures him risen and ascended to the right hand of God, ready to come back in triumph bringing the Last Judgement and a new world order. In his early letters to the churches Paul has great difficulty explaining why Christians were dying before Jesus returned. He gradually realized that the return of Jesus was not going to come as quickly as he expected. By the time St Luke's Gospel was written the return had been postponed into the indefinite future.

Problems with the Second Coming

I have to confess that I have always had a problem with the belief in the Second Coming. If Jesus himself believed it, surely he got it wrong. He did not return. There was not and there is not a manifestly or qualitatively better world. I put this problem to Ed, saying, 'I find it very difficult to understand that people could believe Jesus was the Son of God, as the early Church appeared to believe, and yet accept that he made such a huge mistake – he got his prophecy all wrong.'

Ed replied, 'The people who became Christians were certain that Jesus had been raised from the dead, and that his being raised was a promise to them of everlasting life. When they heard the Christian message and they believed in it, they turned to the God of Israel who had created the world. They also then turned to the Son, as many of them were beginning to believe that Jesus was the Son of God who mediated God's presence to the world. They found a religion of love and truthfulness and mercy and they liked it – there's a lot more to it than "Hold on to your hats, boys, the end is round the corner"!'

'But scholars like you, who say Jesus was a prophet of the Kingdom of God, still seem to be saying this was all there was to it – hold on to your hats and wait for that Kingdom.'

Ed was shocked. 'Oh, goodness, no,' he replied, leaning forward earnestly. 'I wouldn't want to say that's all there was to it. I think that Jesus did expect the end to come, but the Gospels also record the teachings of Jesus, like "love your enemies". He was a very high ethical teacher. He told marvellous parables that give point and meaning to various aspects of existence. No, I don't think that Jesus had only one arrow in his quiver – the expectation that God would intervene in the world. I think he had views about how people ought to live and how they should behave, and he had views about how to be intimate with God and close to him.'

But even if Ed was right about the early Church I still had a problem. I simply could not understand how Jesus could be the Son of God and yet get his message so completely wrong. That was the problem which faced one of the best-known Christians of the last hundred years or so, Albert Schweitzer. After intensive study of all the books he could find on the life of Jesus he came to an even more stark conclusion than Ed Sanders. Schweitzer believed that Jesus thought the Kingdom of God would come immediately, even in his own lifetime, and that when it arrived he would become the Messiah. Having come to this conclusion, Schweitzer did not reinterpret the Kingdom of God in terms of permanent ethical values, as some theologians have done, nor did he soften the concept of the Messiah. He simply said that Jesus got it wrong. Yet, after reaching that conclusion, he gave up an outstandingly successful and happy life as a philosopher, theologian and organist to go and work as a missionary doctor in a French colony in Africa.

Many of Schweitzer's friends tried to dissuade him, saying that he would be wasting his enormous talents. Some even suggested that his motives were suspect: they accused him of wanting to become a hero, or of being disappointed with the level of recognition that his work had received. A few even suspected that he had been unhappy in love. But Schweitzer's explanation was very straightforward. He said, 'The effort to serve the love of Jesus may sweep a man into a new course of love.'

When I came to write this book I searched for an explanation of this apparent contradiction: such a deep love for a historical figure who was apparently deluded. I found this explanation in a book by George Seaver on Schweitzer's life and thought:

> To understand the personality of the historical Jesus, even if only partially
> (for historical investigation can pretend to no more than this) it is necessary

to study him against the background of his own day. This involves the frank recognition that he was subject to the limitations of knowledge incident to his day; a world-view that is to say in which ideas of impending catastrophe to the world-process itself were prevalent. That subsequent history has belied that expectation detracts no whit from his superhuman greatness or from the abiding power of his life, or from the eternal value of his words. In him the eternal is clothed in the temporal, but it is necessary to distinguish the eternal from the temporal.

So Jesus was a man of his times, suffused with the expectation that some great cataclysm was going to take place. If he had not shared that expectation he would have been less than human. Yet at the same time the eternal was in him.

Schweitzer described the failure of Jesus's expectations to materialize as his victory. Some of his most beautiful and best-known words are these:

> There is silence all around. The Baptist appears and cries, 'Repent for the Kingdom of God is at hand.' Soon after that comes Jesus, and in the knowledge that he is the coming Son of Man, lays hold of the wheel of the world to set it moving on that last revolution which is to bring all ordinary history to a close. It refuses to turn and he throws himself upon it. Then it does turn; and crushes him. Instead of bringing in the eschatological conditions, he has destroyed them. The wheel rolls onward, and the mangled body of the one immeasurably great man, who was strong enough to think of himself as the spiritual ruler of mankind and to bend history to his purpose, is hanging upon it still. That is his victory and his reign.

I'm not sure whether I fully understand those words, but I do find one profound meaning in them – in my search for the historical Jesus, Jesus the man, Jesus the Jew, I must not forget that it is history which has shown both that he was a real human being, and that he was at the very least no ordinary man. If he had been there would have been no Church, no two thousand years of Christianity and no Christians devoting their lives to him.

Schweitzer's own life is a reminder of that truth too. Very few scholars would now accept his interpretation of the historical Jesus, and his eschatology has not lasted either. But the power of the life he lived, a life inspired by the uniqueness of Jesus, does survive. It may not necessarily be wrong to say that his life was inspired by the divinity in Jesus.

Pilgrims on the Via Dolorosa

To remind me of the power that Jesus still exercises I joined the Franciscan friars who conduct pilgrims along the Via Dolorosa in Jerusalem every Friday. This was the one pilgrimage I had always wanted to make, because the Crucifixion is for me where Jesus is supremely human, suffering that most brutal form of execution. We have no evidence that God in any way mitigated his suffering. It is this sacrifice which still brings Jesus so close to millions of Christians even though nearly two thousand years have elapsed. The Crucifixion was a historical event, yet at the same time it is shrouded in mystery – the mystery without which I believe there can be no awareness of God.

We were a very varied group of tourists. Some were apparently just curious: a young blonde woman with a short skirt and bare arms, a middle-aged man with a gaudy tee-shirt stretched across his pot-belly, a Japanese couple who were very keen photographers. Some were pilgrims: a party of elderly women wearing yellow and white hats with red crosses on the front, a group of nuns in white habits. There were about twenty Franciscan friars, wearing their brown robes and sandals, who led us into the Old City chanting in Latin. We stopped, and a friar who must have come from the Philippines or some other south-east Asian country took a loudspeaker from one of his colleagues to announce in solemn tones, 'This is the first station where Jesus is condemned to death. Pilate protested, "What crime has he committed?" They only shouted the louder. "Crucify him!"' We moved on again past the second station to the third, where the friar told us Jesus fell for the first time. We entered a covered passageway with shops on either side. The Franciscans were tense and hurried us along. I thought they must be afraid that Muslims or Jews might take offence at this public display of Christianity. But then I learnt that it was the shopkeepers who did not like the entrances to their stores

OVERLEAF
Packed crowds of pilgrims follow the traditional
way of the cross in Jerusalem through streets
marked Via Dolorosa, the road of sorrows.
The devotion of walking through the Stations
of the Cross with prayers and meditations
was started in the Middle Ages.

being blocked. An Arab wearing a red fez with a black tassel appeared. He seemed to be a mediator between the friars and the shopkeepers. A burly young Franciscan with close-cropped black hair and dark glasses, who looked more like a member of the Mafia than a man of God, pushed a party of tourists out of the way to let us get by.

A man protested, 'You pushed me.'

'Yes, and I'll push you again,' snarled the Franciscan, picking the man up and slamming him against the wall.

Shopkeepers intervened. They didn't want the peace to be disturbed.

On we went past the seventh station, where Jesus fell for the second time. As I followed the way which Jesus, according to tradition, followed on that last walk from the 'hall called the praetorium' to the 'place called Golgotha', I thought, 'It doesn't matter whether this was the route he took or not. What matters is the faith of all those pilgrims down the centuries who have trod this way before me.'

We entered the church of the Holy Sepulchre and climbed up the steep, narrow staircase leading to the chapel which marks the spot where Jesus is said to have been crucified. Icons and mosaics glittered in the light of oil lamps and candles. A Greek Orthodox priest stood and watched as the friar who had led our pilgrimage announced, 'The twelfth station. Here Jesus died on the cross.' Then we went down again into the body of the church. The Franciscans, by now holding candles, walked through the dark aisles still chanting in Latin. It was as though we had been carried back to some medieval monastery. I felt that sense of awe and mystery which I only find in traditional worship. We approached the monument built over the tomb of Jesus. In his guidebook Father Jerry had quoted a description of it as 'a hideous kiosk', but I wasn't interested in its artistic merit. I was, I suppose, on a spiritual high by now. The friar announced, 'The fourteenth station. Here Jesus was laid in the tomb.' He then went on to pray. 'Receive our departed brethren, O Jesus, into the heavenly kingdom where with the Father and the Holy Spirit you will be all in all.' I had forgotten Jesus the man by now, but I was intensely aware of Jesus the God. That was perhaps not inappropriate standing in front of the place where Jesus the man was said to have been buried, and to have risen as Christ the Lord. The historical truth did not matter. The myth inspired the conviction that I was experiencing God. Strange that I who had been unmoved by the churches in Galilee, only sensing something of Jesus in the open countryside, should have the most profound experience of my journey to the Holy Land in that church in the centre of old Jerusalem.

Walking in the way of the cross through the tense alleys of the Old City made me aware of the urgency of the question, who killed Jesus? I was always brought up to believe it was the Jews. The Gospels are inconsistent in their accounts of what happened in Jesus's last twenty-four hours, but they all agree that the Jewish authorities were largely responsible. All four Gospels say that the Temple police were involved in the arrest of Jesus. They all say he was taken to the high priest, Caiaphas, and interrogated. Matthew, Mark and Luke add that he was beaten up. These three writers also claim that there was a custom at Passover by which the Roman governor would release a popular prisoner to the crowd. Pilate offers the choice of Jesus or Barabbas, and the priests persuade the crowd to choose Barabbas. When Pilate sees that the crowd are reaching fever pitch he symbolically washes his hands to declare his innocence and then allows the execution of Jesus to proceed. At which 'all the people' respond, 'His blood be on us and on our children.'

The picture in the Gospels is of an angry, envious Jewish establishment plotting to get rid of Jesus, while a detached Roman governor reluctantly agrees to what he sees is an unjust death for the sake of public order. But this picture does not stand up to historical scrutiny. First there is a confusion over what Jesus was actually accused of. Caiaphas finds him guilty of blasphemy, a serious enough crime but not one which would have greatly worried a pagan Roman governor. Curiously, a witness does come forward to report Jesus's prophecy against the Temple, but Matthew describes him as a false witness. The blasphemy charge is not raised with Pilate. Instead Jesus is accused of claiming to be king of the Jews, in other words of subversion. Luke also says he was accused of stirring up the people, perverting the nation and denouncing the tax system. Second, there is a problem about the legal procedures against Jesus. Three of the Gospels say there was a meeting of the Jewish council. Matthew has the council condemning Jesus to death. But there is no evidence that the council had powers to condemn anyone to death. John's acknowledgement of this is closer to history than Matthew's version. Third, it is doubtful whether there was a tradition of releasing a prisoner at the Passover, and it is on this that the Gospel story of Pilate's anxiety to show mercy depends. So one of the best-known stories in the Bible – Pilate washing his hands and saying to the Jewish crowd, 'I am innocent of this righteous

These altars in the church of
the Holy Sepulchre are
believed to be built above
Mount Calvary, the site of
the Crucifixion. Under
the altar on the right
the bare rock can be seen
beneath a glass frame.

man's blood; see to it yourselves' – is probably an interpolation by the Gospel writers to demonstrate that the Romans had no hand in the death of Jesus.

If the Gospel account of the trial is not to be taken at face value, did his fellow Jews have any role in the death of Jesus? At the time of Jesus the Jews were not a composite united people. The Sadducees were the smallest of the Jewish sects and perhaps the furthest removed from the people. Their position did not depend on popular support, as that of the Pharisees did. If a Pharisee's preaching and teaching did not attract a following, he would have no influence. The Sadducees exercised power because they dominated the administration of the Temple, and whether or not they liked the way the Temple was run a large number of Jews regarded it as central to their religion. They believed that they should attend major festivals at the Temple and that the identity of the nation was guaranteed by the continuing office of the high priest and the sacrifices made in the Temple, and they accepted the obligation to pay tribute to the priests.

That position did not, however, go unchallenged. Those in authority had good reason to be nervous. They must have known that the Essenes were critical of the Temple, and many Pharisees were preaching a more personal, spiritualized religion which did not need a physical Temple at its heart. All this was alarming. But only Jesus had actually dared to denounce the Temple, claiming that God would sweep it away and build a new one. For the high priest this prophecy would have been close to blasphemy.

But it was not just because the prophecy challenged the Temple that it was dangerous. Jesus made the prophecy at Passover, when the city was full to bursting and nationalist sentiments were at their height. Normally Pontius Pilate, the Roman governor, lived at Caesarea Philippi, deliberately keeping out of Jerusalem so as not to incite the Jews. He did not intervene in the affairs of the city unless he regarded it as absolutely essential. In this he was simply following Roman policy, which was to respect local religions. Officially, Rome accepted the faith and customs of the Jews and had no desire to overturn them. This was why the Romans ensured that it was the priests with their own guards who policed the Temple and the city. Only at Passover did Pilate come to Jerusalem, bringing soldiers of the Roman Empire with him, because he feared that trouble might break out during the festival. Pilate had good reason to be nervous at Passover, as Ed Sanders explained to me. 'For one thing there was just an enormous crowd on hand. The ordinary population of Jerusalem was perhaps twenty-five thousand or thirty thousand, but for Passover it was about three hundred and fifty thousand – it was packed. Passover was also the celebration of the liberation of Israel from bondage in Egypt, which rather brought to mind the question of foreign oppression and so it was a good time to resent Rome. Passover naturally triggers thoughts of independence.' David Rosen described Passover to me as 'an insidious subversive festival as far as Rome was concerned'.

When Jesus prophesied the destruction of the Temple, the high priest, Caiaphas, and the leading Sadducees and Pharisees who comprised the council were faced with an appalling dilemma. Quite apart from the possibly intended attack on their own privileges, there had been a massacre at Passover in 4 BC. If there were a disturbance as a result of Jesus's prophecy, and if it got out of hand, the Romans themselves might panic and send for reinforcements from Syria. Thousands of Jews might be killed. Caiaphas himself would almost certainly have been dismissed by the Romans, who relied on the high priest to maintain law and order. The high priest and his colleagues must have known that Pilate was unlikely to deal sensitively with any disturbances. We know from other sources that he had a brutal record, and was prone to order mass executions as a way of inspiring terror. He was eventually dismissed for excessive harshness. Pilate was not the rather detached, almost benign figure that the Gospels depict. Of all the Gospels, only John seems to have had some insight into Caiaphas's problem when he reports him as saying, 'It is expedient that one man should die for the people, and that the whole nation should not perish.'

All the indications, therefore, are that the priests did, as the Gospels say, take steps to ensure that Jesus was marked out as a trouble-maker. Pilate would probably not have hesitated in taking firm action against a man whom the high priest said seemed bent on causing a riot.

Convenient scapegoats

So where do the stories about Pilate's attempts to be lenient on Jesus come from? Most scholars believe they are part of a later tradition inserted into the Gospels because the writers wanted the blame for Jesus's Crucifixion to be put on the Jewish authorities. The early Christians were most anxious not to be identified as revolutionaries. They did not want it to be said that they were followers of a rebel against the Roman Empire. All the Gospel writers portray the Romans in a favourable light. It is, for instance, a Roman centurion who, after the Crucifixion, grasps the real identity of Jesus by saying, 'Truly this was the Son of God.'

One of the reasons for the split between Christianity and Judaism was the Church's decision to admit Gentiles. St Paul pressed for this – he was, after all, preaching to Gentiles – but many Jewish Christians were unwilling to contemplate letting Gentiles in without prior conversion to Judaism. The Acts of the Apostles puts the fateful decision at the Council of Jerusalem, which was probably in AD 49. Jewish doubts were not unreasonable.

The Jews were influential and numerous throughout the Roman Empire; the Christians were a small, vulnerable breakaway group. They had to prove they were not a threat to Rome. The famous incident of Pilate washing his hands is intended to demonstrate Roman innocence. It was simply expedient, and understandable, for the Christians to blame the Jews rather than the Romans; as expedient, and understandable, as it had been for Caiaphas to prevent civic violence by arranging the death of Jesus.

At the same time the dispute that arose between Jews and Christians probably influenced the Gospel writers' attitudes too. One of the themes that runs through St John's Gospel is that the Jews were to blame right from the beginning for rejecting Jesus and crucifying him. John places the incident in the Temple at the start of Jesus's ministry to emphasize this very point. The trouble between the two faiths began as a family quarrel within Judaism, and it took nearly two centuries for Christianity to break away from its roots. The first Christians were all Jews: they continued to worship in the synagogues, and at the Temple until it was destroyed. The first Christian community in Jerusalem was run by James, the Lord's brother, and it would have been perceived as a Messianic sect of Judaism rather than as a new religion. But as more and more Gentiles were attracted to the new faith, particularly through St Paul's teaching, tensions between Christians and other Jews increased. Eventually some Jewish communities began to bar Christians from the synagogues. This ban created an enormous bitterness between the two groups, which is reflected in the Gospels. John's Gospel has Jesus prophesying the split on the night before his betrayal: 'They will put you out of the synagogues; indeed the hour is coming when whoever kills you will think he is offering service to God.'

Few scholars believe that the Gospel writers were what we would now call anti-Semitic. Ed Sanders said to me, 'The cry in the Gospel of Matthew, "His blood be on us and on our children", has been used again and again to justify slaughter of Jews, and I'm sure that if Matthew had known the result he would not have written those words.' But as early as the second century Christian theologians were beginning to write tracts against the Jews. Melito of Sardis, a bishop and composer of prayers, accused the Jews of 'deicide', or killing God. In the fourth century St John Chrysostom, one of the greatest of the Fathers of the Eastern Church, known in other contexts for his Christian charity, called Jews 'the murderers of Christ'. St Jerome, revered by Christians for first translating the Bible into Latin, described Jewish pilgrims in Jerusalem as 'hordes of wretches, not worthy of pity . . . their very exterior and clothes betraying the wrath of God'. St Augustine, whose thinking dominated the theology of the Western Church for almost eight hundred years, repeated the charge that the Jews had killed God, and also expressed the belief that the Jews would continue to be punished for their crime. He was followed down the centuries by many leading Christian teachers including Gregory the Great, known as the father of the medieval papacy, and the Protestant reformer Martin Luther. It became an orthodox tenet of Christianity that the scattering of the Jews throughout the world was God's punishment for killing his son – a tenet that lived on to the twentieth century. The founder of the Zionist Movement, Theodore Herzl, argued that the only alternative to persecution was to found a Jewish state. In 1897 the first World Zionist Congress was held in Basle. The Zionists gained many sympathizers, among them Lord Balfour, the British Foreign Secretary, who in 1917 persuaded the Government to promise Zionists a national home in Palestine. The Jesuit paper *La Civiltà Cattolica* rejected this on the grounds that it would contravene the divine curse on the Jews. They had been condemned to wander for ever.

Synods and Councils of the Church legalized what should surely have been seen as un-Christian behaviour to the Jews. As early as AD 306 the Synod of Elvira prohibited marriage or sexual intercourse between Christians and Jews. Among later prohibitions were bans on Jews holding public office, employing Christian servants and appearing in court cases as witnesses against Christians. The Synod of Geneva in 1078 ordered Jews to pay taxes to support the Church. The Council of Oxford, some one hundred and fifty years later, banned the building of new synagogues. In 1267 the Synod of Breslau obliged Jews to live in ghettos. It wasn't until the Second Vatican Council in 1965 that the Roman Catholic Church formally absolved the Jews now living of killing Jesus. The Council stated that the Crucifixion should not be charged against all Jews without distinction then alive, nor against the Jews of today. It took the Nazi Holocaust against the Jews to achieve that.

The terrible legacy

In Jerusalem I visited Yad Vashem, the hall set in a park where the eternal flame burns in memory of the millions of Jews killed in the Holocaust. On the floor are inscribed the names of the camps where terrible atrocities occurred – Bergen-Belsen, Buchenwald, Dachau, Ravensbruck and many others. At Auschwitz twelve thousand Jewish children and old men were killed in gas chambers every day, herded to their death like animals in a slaughterhouse. More than two million Jews were murdered there alone between 1941 and 1944. The able-bodied men were sent to slave labour camps, where many died. This was part of Hitler's 'final solution of the Jewish question'. The intention was to round up all Jews and send them to concentration camps. The unfit were to be exterminated, the able-bodied were to be worked to death. It was a coolly planned and efficiently executed attempt at genocide which came all too near to total success. No one will ever know exactly how many Jews were killed, although it can be said with some accuracy that during the war their numbers declined by about six million – two-thirds of the Jewish population in Europe.

As I looked at the names of those camps I remembered the reports I had read of the horrifying discoveries that the Allied armies made when they entered the concentration camps – starving survivors, piles of corpses, the ashes of countless bodies which had been cremated, warehouses full of personal possessions, even shoes and spectacles, evidence of sterilization and painful, often lethal, medical experiments on human guinea pigs. I wondered, 'Could all this have happened if Christians had not been taught to hate the Jews for killing Jesus?'

No event in history can be explained as simply as that. Economic circumstances made the Jews the obvious scapegoats that Hitler needed to arouse the anger of the German people, to create the hysteria necessary to spread fascism. It was the fear, the despair, and above all else the anger of the German people faced with the collapse of their economy which made Hitler such an effective orator. That was made clear by a German eye-witness who described one of Hitler's rallies:

> I looked round at the audience. Where was the nondescript crowd I had seen only an hour before? What was suddenly holding these people who, on the hopeless incline of the falling mark, were engaged in a daily struggle to keep themselves within the line of decency? The hubbub and the mug-clattering had stopped, and they were drinking in every word. Only a few yards away was a young woman, her eyes fastened on the speaker. Transfixed as though in some devotional ecstasy, she had ceased to be herself, and was completely under the spell of Hitler's despotic faith in Germany's future greatness.

Nationalism feeds on hatred, and the Jews were the obvious target for Hitler to choose. He loathed Jews himself, and he knew that many of his fellow countrymen did too. The Jews had only been freed from their ghettos some fifty years earlier, but many of them had prospered in that short time. They became particularly prominent in commerce and industry, opening department stores and starting new industries remarkable for the revolutionary technology they employed. It was all too easy for Hitler to blame these prosperous Jews, carrying the burden of centuries of hatred, for the collapse of the mark, to accuse them of black-marketeering in the first World War, and of making money out of the present misfortunes of the people. He could also accuse them of being in league with the communists, the enemies of German nationalism. After all, Karl Marx was a Jew.

But perhaps there is another aspect to the Holocaust which makes it so horrific. It is only in our century that technology has become sophisticated enough for us to destroy a whole people in the anonymous, mechanical way of the death camps. Many ordinary Germans at Auschwitz and Dachau believed they were just doing their job. Like factory workers, they did what their supervisors said without feeling personally involved. The Holocaust

---

OVERLEAF
The countless Jewish children slaughtered
in the Holocaust are remembered in
the Yad Vashem children's memorial.

raises questions about our basic humanity. It has shown us the spiritual dangers of 'hi-tech', and exposed the lies that are involved in politicians' talk of smart, clean, efficient weapons. At least until modern times, in order to kill an enemy you had to look into his face. It is because the Holocaust threatens the humanity of all of us that Jewish writers and thinkers are so determined that we should not forget either the horror itself or the history that contributed to it. Yad Vashem is one attempt to make sure we do not.

When I was at Yad Vashem I met an Englishwoman, Joanna Ryam, a Christian by birth and upbringing but now a Jew living in Israel. She told me, 'There was a moment at which I decided I wanted to become a Jew, and that was after living here for about eight years. As I came to discover and understand the Holocaust I could no longer identify with being a Christian.'

I asked her, 'To what extent do you think anti-Semitism springs from the historic misconception that the Jews as a race crucified Jesus?'

She thought for a moment before answering, 'That's what I was taught. I was educated at a Catholic convent.'

'They clearly said that the Jews were the enemies of Jesus?'

'Yes, and responsible for his death. Obviously I've read quite a bit since I've been here and looked at it in much greater detail, and it does seem to be the wellspring of anti-Semitism.'

Joanna Ryam suggested that we should walk down to the other Holocaust Memorial, the Valley of the Communities. We walked along the paths cut through the red rocks and read the names of the communities which had suffered in the Holocaust. I was amazed. Jews had been killed in Norway and Finland in the north, in France in the west, on the shores of the Black Sea in the east, and as far south as Libya. I had never realized that the Holocaust had spread so far. Joanna reminded me that an estimated one million Jews had been killed during the German advance into the Soviet Union. In part, at least, the blame must lie at the door of Christianity which has propagated a story of Jesus's Crucifixion that is historically improbable.

3

Jesus the Rebel

In Palestine

P alestine is not just the Holy Land, it is the bridge between Asia and Africa, trodden by travellers and fought over down the centuries. This makes it an archaeologists' paradise. In the introduction to his guidebook Father Jerry mentions part of a human skeleton found in Palestine which is believed to be six hundred thousand years old.

One of the most spectacular of the thousands of archaeological sites in Palestine is Beth Shean. Archaeologists have discovered that no fewer than eighteen cities were built on this site, taking advantage of an abundance of water in a strategically important but dry and barren area. Beth-shan was the city where, according to the first Book of Samuel, the Philistines 'fastened' the body of Israel's first king, Saul, to the wall after defeating him in the battle of Mount Gilboa. David, who was to be the next king, heard that Saul's son, his beloved friend Jonathan, had been killed in the battle. This led him to pour out his grief in one of the best known of all lamentations: 'I am distressed for you, my brother Jonathan; very pleasant have you been to me; your love to me was wonderful, passing the love of women. How are the mighty fallen and the weapons of war perished!'

Beth Shean is now dominated by the remains of the city that the Romans

OVERLEAF
Ruins of the Roman settlement at Beth Shean. Though this city was built after the time of Jesus, it reveals the cultural dominance of the Romans in Galilee. Jesus grew up in Nazareth, near the Roman city of Sepphoris.

constructed, and the Byzantine city which succeeded it. Much of the vast area is strewn with ruins, and extensive work is going on to try to restore parts of these cities. It was at Beth Shean that I met the New Testament scholar who was to introduce me to Jesus the rebel, Richard Horsley, Professor of Religion at the University of Massachusetts in Boston. He was a small man with a shock of white hair which somehow did not detract from the youthfulness of his face. This was his first visit to the Holy Land, and he leaped around the vast archaeological dig like an excited schoolboy, delighted to see with his own eyes evidence of the magnificence and splendour of the Roman cities which he believed had such an impact on the subject Jews of Jesus's time. Pointing to the sturdy stone pillars, some lying strewn on the ground, others being re-erected by cranes as we talked, he said, 'When the Romans came it wasn't just a military imperialism they imposed, it was also a cultural imperialism. These monumental columns were really a form of propaganda that was designed to intimidate the populace just by the sheer magnitude of the construction. The aim was to overwhelm the people with the sheer size of the buildings.'

That is not to deny the military purpose of the settlement. As Richard Horsley pointed out to me, this was the base from which the Roman legions moved up into eastern Galilee to stamp out peasant resistance during the Jewish War against the Romans which broke out in AD 66.

Eventually we reached the amphitheatre which once accommodated audiences of five thousand. It has survived comparatively intact, having lost only the upper tiers of its steeply banked seating. I asked Richard Horsley how the Jews would have reacted to the entertainment provided there, and he told me, 'Here in the amphitheatre they would have been exercising in the nude, there would have been games with beasts, and all such things would have been scandalous to Jewish culture. Let's also remember the economic exploitations which would have funded such entertainments, the economic exploitation of the indigenous population which supported the city, and the other layers of taxation supporting the Roman troops that would have been based here.'

By the time the Romans came to Palestine Jewish culture had survived many assaults. The Romans were the last of many conquerors. First there were the Assyrians, eight hundred years earlier, then the Babylonians, who sacked Jerusalem, then the Persians, then Alexander the Great. It was under Alexander that the Jews were first exposed to Greek culture, which disgusted them with its theatres and sports as much as the Roman games did later. For a short while Palestine was a vassal of Egypt before being taken over by a new empire – that of the Seleucids who had come to power in the wake of Alexander the Great and ruled Northern Syria and Persia. At first the Jews were well treated by these new overlords, but there was mounting pressure to accept pagan habits. Even some of the high priests accepted a relaxing of the food laws and tolerated idolatry. One particularly insensitive Seleucid king, Antiochus Epiphanes, tried to force the Jews to abandon their traditions altogether. This sparked off a revolt. The king responded by desecrating the Temple in Jerusalem. On 25 Chislev (December) in the year 168 or 167 BC – no one is sure which – pigs were offered in sacrifice on an altar to the Greek god Zeus. The Jews rose up in violent rebellion, the Seleucid army was

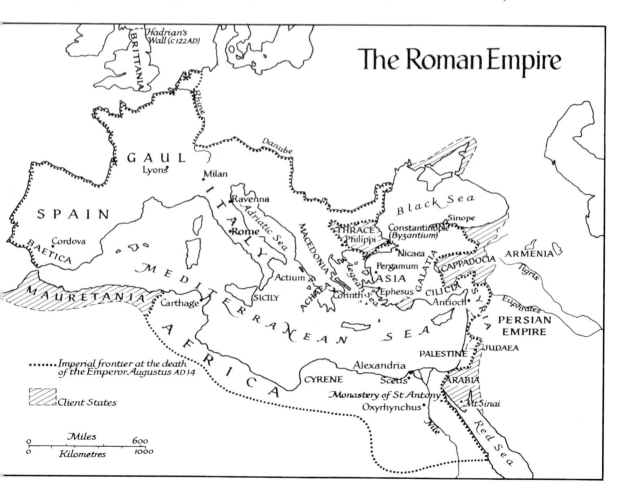

The Roman Empire

Imperial frontier at the death
of the Emperor Augustus AD 14

Client States

Miles 600
Kilometres 1000

defeated and the Temple was cleansed and rededicated. This was the start of a period of rule by Maccabean priests and a hundred years of freedom for the Jews – freedom ended by the Roman warlord Pompey in 63 BC.

The years before the birth of Jesus saw the Roman world split by civil war. Julius Caesar was Rome's greatest military leader and wanted to take supreme power, but he was opposed by Pompey. The Egyptian queen Cleopatra did her best to play the one off against the other. Caesar eventually crossed the Rubicon and invaded Italy, ruling Rome until he was assassinated. Civil war did not end until Augustus established himself as emperor in 30 BC. The comparative peace he brought and the empire he founded, with its cities and roads and sophisticated communications, played a crucial role in the spread of Christianity.

Heavy taxes, ruined lives

Remembering Father Jerry's suggestion that Joseph came to Nazareth to find work on the rebuilding of the city of Sepphoris, I suggested to Horsley that the cities could not have been a burden to all the local population as they would have provided work for some. In India, for instance, many great monuments, including the Taj Mahal, were built to provide work during times of famine. But Horsley disagreed totally. 'The drain was one-way, just like the aqueduct which brought water into the city. The system worked in such a way as to take the produce from the country and bring it into the granaries, from where it was used to support the people who really supported the king – the artisans who made his fancy hangings, the builders who built his fancy buildings, and the army that kept him secure.' Having studied the economic history of Jesus's times, Richard Horsley interprets the Gospels as the story of a rebel who was telling the villagers of Galilee to stand together and act together, so that they could resist the government of the Romans and their client kings.

The writings of the Jewish historian Josephus are the basis for Professor Horsley's research. Josephus was born and brought up in Palestine and played a leading part in the last revolt of the Jews against the Romans, which occurred forty years after the death of Jesus and ended with the destruction of the Temple in AD 70. Josephus was taken prisoner and sent to Rome, but he so impressed his captors that they gave him an imperial pension. This enabled him to write his detailed history of the Jewish War, in which he carefully discounted anything that would offend the Romans. For this reason modern historians used to discount Josephus's picture of Jewish life, but Horsley believes he gives an accurate enough picture, even though he was writing for Roman consumption. Josephus shows us that the Palestine of Jesus's time – the years which led up the Jewish war – was far from peaceful. Oppression, violence and banditry were rife. The causes, according to Horsley, were economic.

Horsley does not just rely on Josephus. He believes that we only obtain a true picture of Jesus if we look at the social history of his times. He has tried to understand Jesus's era by looking at what happens in other peasant societies when they become subject to a greater power. The greatest problem is that they have to fit in with the economic interests of their overlords. The chief economic interest of the Romans was feeding their population: they needed bread, and looked to their subject states to provide it. Big farms were more useful than small farms, so there was economic pressure against the peasant farmer. This was particularly difficult to accept because the Jewish tradition was that the land was God's possession, to be used for the benefit of all.

The people of Galilee laboured under the burden of three taxes, one levied by the Romans, one by the king, and one by the Temple authorities in Jerusalem. This heavy taxation, Horsley believes, was driving many small-holders into debt and forcing them to sell their land. That probably meant more than losing their livelihood, which was bad enough. Jews who lost their land and had to beg, or live by getting whatever work they could each day, were regarded as little better than outcasts. Murderers, thieves, extortioners and prostitutes, as well as those involved in organizing gambling, those who had purchased the right to collect taxes, and those who lent money and charged interest were all officially classified as outcasts by Orthodox Jews. According to Marcus Borg, the outcasts were regarded as 'virtually untouchables, not very different from the lowest caste of the Hindu system, though the status of outcast was not hereditary in Judaism'.

So the heavy taxation and the indebtedness which came with it threatened peasant farmers not just with economic ruin but with ostracism from their community too. It is difficult for those who live in comparatively fluid industrial societies to realize what loss of status means in a static, structured, agrarian society. Horsley told me he thought that if Joseph was, as tradition has it, a carpenter, then Jesus too came from a family of 'downwardly mobile peasants'. He saw a carpenter as an artisan who had lost his land, possibly because of his debts, and had to earn his living in another way. If this was true of Jesus's family, it would have made him very sensitive to the problem of debt and loss of land that Horsley believes was endemic at the time.

Political and social reformer

This interpretation differs from Father Jerry's concept of a Jesus brought up in a cosmopolitan background, the child of a poor but reasonably secure home. Which picture is true seems to me to depend on whether Joseph was a skilled carpenter or just a labourer on a building site. In most traditional societies a skilled carpenter is by no means at the bottom of the social scale, and has considerable pride in his craft. He passes his skill on to his sons, and so the family has a stable income so long as there is a demand for carpentry. The building activity in Galilee at the time would have created that demand. So there are also arguments against Jesus coming from a 'downwardly mobile' family.

Whether Jesus's family was teetering on the brink between respectability and outcast status or not, there seems little doubt that times were hard and that debt was a major social problem. Traditional scholarship has tended to ignore the economic circumstances in Galilee, concentrating on comparing the Gospel texts with each other and with other relevant literature – in particular the Old Testament, the writings of the rabbis after the destruction of the Temple in AD 70, and the Dead Sea Scrolls. This concentration on texts has created the impression that Jesus was preaching a purely religious message, appealing for repentance and a new awareness of God. Horsley believes that the message Jesus preached was a social message.

One of the sites in Galilee much visited by Christian pilgrims is the church of the Beatitudes. This, pilgrims are told, is the mount on which Jesus preached the world's most famous sermon. The church, built as recently as 1938, is classical in style, an eight-sided structure supporting a dome. The eight sides represent the eight Beatitudes. It is not remarkable for its beauty, but its setting is magnificent. As I looked down on the bright blue Sea of Galilee, glittering in the sunlight, I could see almost all the places where Jesus is believed to have ministered and taught. The Sermon on the Mount has been regarded by Christians as the supreme spiritual teaching of Jesus. Many non-Christians, including Mahatma Gandhi, have had an enormous respect for its message. The Beatitudes have been the subject of innumerable sermons exhorting Christians to be humble, to be merciful, to be generous, to strive to be righteous – in summary, to lead virtuous and godly lives. Those sermons have interpreted the Beatitudes as spiritual teaching.

Horsley considers that interpretation to be too narrow. He maintains that the Beatitudes contain a political message too, and has written, 'we should assume that Jesus's preaching and practice referred to the several inseparable dimensions of life unless a passage gives a clear indication that only a "spiritual" or "religious" dimension is intended. Reaffirming this principle is particularly important in application to passages such as the Beatitudes which may already have been somewhat spiritualized in the Gospels.' In other words, the Gospel writers have put a religious slant on the Beatitudes which has obscured the political content of their message. Horsley points out, for instance, that St Matthew quoted Jesus as saying, 'Blessed are the poor in spirit', while St Luke just says, 'Blessed are you poor'. St Luke only said, 'Blessed are you that hunger now', while St Matthew adds, 'and thirst after righteousness'. Horsley believes that if you see through the spiritual spin that Matthew in particular has put on the Beatitudes you will share his conclusion that Jesus was talking about those who were economically poor, not those who were righteous because they were humble. It was those who had fallen into the debt trap, those who did not have enough food for just one square meal a day, who Jesus promised would be the beneficiaries of the Kingdom of God. The Kingdom of God, according to Horsley, was to be 'social-economic liberation' – that is to say, freedom from poverty, oppression and social stigma.

The Lord's Prayer is, of course, even better known than the Beatitudes. It has been part of Christian worship from earliest times. It is repeated every time a Roman Catholic priest says the mass, every time a monk or nun says the divine office. It is included in the three main services of the Anglican prayer book, Holy Communion, Matins and Evensong. It is the personal prayer of Catholic, Protestant and Orthodox Christians everywhere. I was taught to think of it as a very personal prayer, with two basic themes. The first was an acknowledgement of the supremacy of God, 'Our Father who art in Heaven, hallowed be thy name', and 'thine is the kingdom, the power and the glory, for ever and ever'. The second was that we needed God's help to live at all and in particular to live a good life: 'Give us this day our daily bread, forgive us our trespasses as we forgive them that trespass against us, and lead us not into temptation, but deliver us from evil.'

Richard Horsley interprets the Lord's Prayer as part of Jesus's political message. Here again he believes the Gospel writers have put a spiritual spin on what he thinks was a straightforward appeal to release those about to fall into poverty as a result of their debts. He points out that in St Matthew's Gospel the words are 'forgive our debts as we forgive our debtors'. So Jesus was telling the Galileans not to drive each other into bankruptcy by insisting on the repayment of debts. St Matthew does quote Jesus as saying after the Our Father, 'For if you forgive men their trespasses, your heavenly father will also forgive you.' But Horsley argues that the only other places where the word 'trespasses' occurs in the Gospels are agreed by scholars to be later additions, not the words of Jesus. In other words, Horsley believes it is another example of Matthew putting a spiritual spin on the original down-to-earth words of Jesus.

When Jesus talked of loving your enemies Horsley believes he was being practical too. He was urging people not to bear grudges, not to let hatred fester. Horsley turns to social studies of other oppressed societies to show how important this teaching must have been. When people are subjected to a harsh rule which does not allow them to give vent to their frustrations they become fractious, suspecting each other as much as they suspect the agents of the government. So quarrels between villagers which led to long-lasting vendettas could have been a serious social problem in Jesus's time. They would have undermined the stable and harmonious society in Galilee which Horsley believes Jesus was trying to establish as a firm base on which to build resistance against the oppressors.

A new view on family relationships

Horsley does not believe it ends there. He thinks Jesus wanted Galileans to do more than change their attitude to each other. He wanted, apparently, to change society so that it was no longer patriarchal. Life was not to be dominated by fathers of families and village elders, but should be freer, with much greater equality. Horsley says that this is the only explanation for Jesus's attitude towards the family.

Jesus seems to have been aware that the urgency of his message could change family relationships. He said, for instance, 'I have come to set a man against his father, and a daughter against her mother, and a daughter-in-law against her mother-in-law; and a man's foes shall be those of his own household.' For centuries most Christians believed that celibacy was superior to marriage, but nowadays the Church teaches that Jesus stood for family values, which of course include harmony. So it has difficulties with Jesus's teaching about strife in the home. Horsley thinks that Jesus was deliberately setting the generations against the generations to break down the patriarchal hierarchy and to end the domination of the male head of the family. He insists that setting a man against his father does not mean that Jesus wanted to break up families.

If Jesus was critical of the patriarchal family, it seems strange that he took a very hard line on divorce. Among Jews of his time there were rabbis who taught that divorce should be easy and others who more or less forbade it. Jesus forbade it. According to St Luke he said: 'Everyone who divorces his wife and marries another commits adultery, and he who marries a woman divorced from her husband commits adultery.' Horsley does not simply interpret Jesus's opposition to divorce as a defence of the family; he uses it to bolster another argument in favour of his theory that Jesus was calling for a less patriarchal society. Traditionally a man could divorce his wife 'if she finds no favour in his eyes because he has found some indecency in her'. All a man had to do was to write a bill of divorce and give it to her; then she could be turned out of the house. In adopting a strict line, Horsley argues, Jesus was taking a stand for women, protecting them from arbitrary divorce and the wretched life that would follow.

There is no evidence that Jesus himself was ever married. This used to be thought strange because family life, and especially children, are so important to Jews. Yet we now know that there were other Jews, like the Dead Sea community at Qumran, who lived as celibates, at least for part of their lives. But whatever the reason for his not marrying, a number of scholars who would not necessarily agree with Horsley's political interpretation of Jesus's message believe that his attitude towards women was remarkably enlightened for his times.

Women do not play a significant role in traditional Judaism. Even today an Orthodox Jewish man will include in his morning prayers the words. 'Blessed art thou O Lord who has not made me a woman.' Women were certainly at a disadvantage in Jesus's time, subject to stringent purity laws which excluded them from society. There is a long tradition of Jewish writing in which women are seen as dangerous temptresses. The Proverbs warn against loose women, singers and entertainers. It is a mistake to get drunk with a woman, or to be beguiled by beauty. Paranoia about women is a common feature of male-dominated religions which put a high premium on sexual purity, so it is not surprising that in the Dead Sea Scrolls there is a poem warning against harlots which bristles with fear.

> *Her heart is set up as a snare,*
> *and her kidneys as*
> *a fowler's net,*
> *Her eyes are defiled with iniquity,*
> *her hands have seized hold of the Pit.*
> *Her legs go down to work wickedness . . .*
> *and a multitude of sins is in her skirt.*
> *She lifts her eye naughtily*
> *to stare at a virtuous one and join him,*
> *and an important one to trip him up,*
> *at upright men to pervert their way,*
> *and the righteous elect to keep them from the commandment,*
> *at the firmly established to bring them down wantonly,*
> *and those who walk in uprightness to alter the statute.*
> *To cause the humble to rebel against God,*
> *and turn their steps away from the ways of justice,*
> *to bring insolence to their heart,*
> *so that they march no more in the paths of uprightness,*
> *to lead men astray to the ways of the pit,*
> *and seduce with flattery every son of man.*

Compare the fear of women as temptresses in that poem with Jesus's attitude.

He healed a woman who was regarded as impure because she had a permanent haemorrhage. He spoke freely to the woman who came to draw water at Jacob's well. He healed the daughter of a ruler of the synagogue. He restored a dead son to the widow of Nain – widows without sons to look after them were obviously particularly vulnerable in a society which gave women little independence. He forgave the woman taken in adultery, rounding angrily on the men who were about to stone her to death.

Women travelled with Jesus as he moved from place to place during his mission. In St Matthew's Gospel we are told that many women followed him all the way from Galilee to Jerusalem on his last journey. He stayed regularly with Martha and Mary, and when Martha asked for his support because she was performing the traditional women's role in the home he backed Mary, who was flouting convention by talking freely to a man. In St Mark's Gospel, when a woman anointed Jesus with very precious oil, he said, 'Truly, I say to you, wherever the Gospel is preached in the whole world what she has done will be told in memory of her.' That was the highest commendation given by Jesus to anyone in the Gospel stories. Jesus seems to have had an especially close relationship with Mary of Magdala, who became one of the first witnesses of the Resurrection. The early Church Fathers declared Mary Magdalene to be 'the Apostle to the Apostles', and the early Church followed Jesus's example in allowing women a much higher status than they enjoyed in normal Jewish society. But it was not long before a male-dominated hierarchy emerged. It has taken nearly two thousand years for Christians to challenge that hierarchy effectively, and there are many battles still to be fought.

Leaving the politics to God

Back in Jerusalem I met Richard Horsley again in the Cardo, a Roman street in the Old City. I needed to clear up in my own mind what sort of revolution the rebel Jesus was planning. The simmering resentment against the Romans and their client kings had spawned small groups who these days would be called terrorists. So I started by asking Horsley whether Jesus would have supported terrorism. To my surprise he replied, 'The interesting thing is that we have nothing to indicate that Jesus would have been against terrorism. We have this whole tradition, including people like myself who are pacifists and base our pacifism on the sayings of Jesus about loving your enemy. But if we look at the original situation addressed by those sayings, they are local social-economic relations. Love your enemy, do good and lend, turn the other cheek. Jesus is referring to local spats among people who probably are in debt to each other. That set of sayings does not refer to action against the Romans. Nor are they telling people not to take action against Herod Antipas. There's nothing to indicate that Jesus would have opposed violence.'

The sayings of Jesus in St Luke's Gospel, 'Love your enemies, do good to those who hate you, bless those who curse you, pray for those who abuse you' have often been interpreted as an early version of Mahatma Gandhi's doctrine of non-violent resistance, and indeed the Mahatma himself admitted to drawing some of his inspiration from the Gospels. Horsley, however, points out that there is no reference to political enemies in these sayings, whether those enemies are people who unjustly repress their own fellow countrymen or foreign oppressors. The references are to personal relationships, and even there Horsley does not find violence is an issue. As he puts it, 'Non-violence is neither the issue nor the message of these sayings.'

But Palestine was a particularly troublesome place as far as the Romans were concerned. Josephus tells us about groups of violent bandits who lived in the wilderness of Judaea and disrupted life for both the Romans and their fellow countrymen. There was a revolt after Herod died. In the first century, during Jesus's lifetime, a man named Ezekias, known as the chief bandit, and his son and grandsons led revolts against Rome. Two of the grandsons were crucified. A third grandson entered the Temple dressed as a king at the start of the great revolution in AD 66. Ezekias's nephew led the resistance to the Romans after the fall of Jerusalem. One scholar has said that all the revolutionary movements which so troubled the Romans stemmed from Galilee. I asked Horsley what Jesus's reaction to these movements would have been.

'Jesus and others may well have been quite aware that it would be suicidal to carry out a massive revolt. They'd already experienced Roman retaliation in AD 4, when revolutionaries broke into the royal armoury in Sepphoris after Herod died. We know from studies of other peasant societies that there are means of resistance short of taking arms. You can lie about your resources, you can hide the grain before the tax collectors get there, there are all sorts of passive resistance that peasants can engage in when their communities have strengthened themselves. Then the rulers can't do a thing about what they really want to get the peasants to do.'

So Horsley's rebel Jesus didn't actually address the question which still perplexes us so much: when, if ever, is it right to take up arms? He apparently relied on God to overthrow the Jews' oppressor. When I asked Horsley to tell me exactly what sort of revolutionary Jesus was he replied, 'I would say Jesus was a revolutionary, but I would put a twist on that. He thought God was taking care of the political revolution, as did many Jews at the time. They believed God was going to take action to remove the Romans from the overlordship here in Palestine. Jesus was active in pursuing what I call a social revolution, where he was encouraging people to get their act together locally and to be strong in those independent village communities. Then in their strength they could all better resist that foreign rule.'

'So Jesus got it wrong because God didn't take care of that political revolution? In fact the Jews were smashed by the Romans about thirty years later, weren't they?'

'I suppose we could say that Jesus got it wrong if we take it narrowly. But, after all, that movement continued and, beside those villages in Galilee having being revitalized, there was a whole movement that spread out beyond Palestine that was touched off by this movement that Jesus started.'

It still seemed to me that I was facing the same problem discussing Jesus the rebel as I had faced with Jesus the eschatological prophet. How did the Jesus movement survive? How did the Church come about when Jesus himself apparently got it wrong?

The importance of the Resurrection

There is one obvious answer to that. Something happened after the Crucifixion which revived Jesus's followers' confidence in their leader. The Crucifixion itself was almost certainly seen by his followers as the end of the movement they had joined, the ultimate failure. Realizing that their lives were in danger they would probably have gone into hiding, hoping that they could eventually get back to their villages and resume their lives. The Gospels do not attempt to hide the failure; they report Peter's denial and the disciples deserting Jesus on the cross.

But then comes the Resurrection: Jesus appears to his followers after the Crucifixion, and morale revives. The resurrected Jesus was not instantly recognized; Mary Magdalene mistook him for a gardener, and the disciples on the road to Emmaus talked with him for hours before he broke bread with them and they realized who he was. Although the visions were very diverse and happened in different places and to different people, they do show a pattern. Fear and grief turned to bewilderment, and then to recognition and joy. Those who dismiss the Resurrection as an impossibility have first to explain why his followers would have made such a claim. There were others who said they were the Messiah and were executed, but there is no record of their followers claiming that the would-be Messiahs had returned from death. Many Jews believed in the resurrection of the body, but they did not think that individuals would from time to time, or as soon as they died, be resurrected. They thought there would be what I might call a mass resurrection on the great day when God judged the world. So while Jesus's followers, being Jews, might have expected the Resurrection at some unknown time in the future, when he was crucified they would not have been expecting to see him alive again.

If Jesus's followers did not believe he had reappeared, why would they have started preaching the Resurrection? There is little doubt that belief in this unusual resurrection goes back to the early days of the Church. Within a few years of Jesus's death St Paul was preaching the Resurrection as an established fact. He was convinced that Jesus had been seen after his death by about five hundred 'brethren' at one time. Most of those 'brethren' were still alive at the time he was writing to the Church in Corinth.

St Paul, perhaps the most effective missionary ever, would not have been prepared to lay down his life for a lie. If those who told Paul about the Resurrection were liars, we have to believe that liars could found a movement which had an immediate and profound impact and which has lasted until today. The New Testament scholar Tom Wright, who taught at Oxford and is now the Dean of Lichfield, argues that although the Resurrection is a problem for our modern minds, 'in the light of the Resurrection we are called to be sceptical about scepticism itself.'

I discussed this with Ed Sanders, asking him how important the Resurrection was to the early Church.

He replied, 'It was absolutely necessary for Christianity. It's the thing that made the Christian faith happen, the motor that drives it. It's indispensable.'

'But what *did* happen?'

'Now that I don't know. I think that with regard to whether or not there was a resurrection we can say this. Either the disciples experienced what they called resurrection, still not defining what that means, or they were all frauds.

Now some of these men were going to give their lives for this faith. I don't think the theories of fraud and mass delusion and so on work very well, so I'm happy to say that the resurrection experiences happened.'

But that left me far from satisfied. I wanted to know what Ed thought *had* happened, what the disciples really experienced. So I asked, 'Why don't you define the Resurrection?'

He replied, 'There we run into terrible problems with the evidence. Anyone can sit down with the end of Matthew, the end of Luke, the end of John, and Chapter 15 of St Paul's Epistle to the Corinthians and write down a list of those to whom Jesus is said to have appeared, and where, and find they are incompatible. So it's impossible to look at these competing stories and then say, "I know for sure what happened". But a couple of negatives come across clearly, things that the Christians who believed in the Resurrection wanted to make sure were excluded. One of them is that the resurrected Lord was a badly wounded man, or a corpse who had gotten a brief dose of new life and could get up and stagger around for a bit but who was very definitely the very same person who had been crucified. For instance, in Luke, Jesus talked to two disciples and they didn't recognize him. According to Paul the Resurrection body was not of flesh and blood. It was a body, but it wasn't flesh and blood. It was transformed, in the same way that Paul thought believers' bodies would be transformed. So the New Testament itself is rather against the notion of a walking corpse or a badly wounded man who only appeared to have died.'

'Is there any other explanation that the New Testament is against?'

'The other thing they're against is the idea that it was a ghost. Ghosts were known in the ancient world, but Christians were dead set against the notion that the resurrected Lord was a ghost. So if ghosts are out, what you are left with is St Paul's phrase for what it was he saw, "a spiritual body". Now I've told you what they experienced. You tell me what that was.'

'All I can tell you, Ed, is that I've never seen a spiritual body.'

We both laughed and Ed said, 'You have never seen one, I have never seen one. Precisely. No, they didn't have the words for it. They didn't have the concepts, or the vocabulary, for what had happened to them.'

'Could there have been a Church if it hadn't happened?'

'I don't think there would have been, no. I think they might have constituted a group within Judaism for a little while, but I don't think Chris-

tianity would have become a worldwide religion, distinct from Judaism, without the Resurrection.'

I have to admit that I was convinced by Ed Sanders. It had always seemed to me that the most certain miracle of Christianity, the one which I found undeniable, was the emergence of the Church. How did men and women whose whole world must have collapsed when Jesus was crucified, who would certainly have been terrified, who had shown neither great courage nor leadership qualities when Jesus was alive, lead a movement which spread so rapidly? There was no mass media to broadcast the message in those days. It had to be carried by hard slogging, often on foot. Yet the message travelled far and wide within the first generation of Christians.

Tradition has it that Christianity quickly became so well established in Rome, the imperial capital, that the authorities thought it necessary to execute the two most prominent first-generation leaders of the Church, Peter and Paul. There is evidence that there might have been riots between Jews and Christians in Rome as early as AD 50, less than twenty years after Jesus died. Fourteen years later the Christian community was sufficiently prominent in the capital for the Emperor Nero to use them as scapegoats for the great fire of AD 64. By the end of the first century – that is, within seventy years of Jesus's death – the Church had spread from Cyrenaica on the African coast of the Mediterranean, all round the eastern rim of the Mediterranean, through what is today Turkey, and through Greece, to Rome in the west of Italy.

The making of a major religious figure

I was frankly delighted that a scholar of the distinction of Ed Sanders seemed to agree with me about the importance of the Resurrection. But it did not seem to me that this explanation would fit in with Horsley's social revolutionary Jesus, and that for me was a weakness of his theory. But like a good journalist I had to listen to all sides of the argument and so I gave Richard

William Blake's depiction of the Angel of the Resurrection rolling the stone away from the entrance of the tomb, while the accompanying angels remove the grave-clothes from the dazzled-looking Jesus.

Horsley, who of course has a considerable reputation as a scholar too, a chance to have his say. I asked him, 'How do you make the jump from your concept of Jesus the social revolutionary in a very remote part of Palestine to what Jesus very soon became, a major religious figure?'

Horsley replied, 'Well, it's not as simple as it's portrayed in the Acts of the Apostles, which of course was written two or three generations later. If we look at our earliest records it's clear that there were actually several communities which emerged from Jesus's ministry, and not all of them emphasize the resurrection. In fact not all of them place quite the explicit emphasis on the Crucifixion as do others. If we read the documents from some of these movements, it looks as though they are coming out of Israelite prophetic traditions where Jesus is the last and greatest in the line of the prophets. He's now become a martyr to his cause. They were communities which tried to continue that line of the prophetic tradition, by continuing Jesus's cause as a community of the renewed Israel.'

I thought as he spoke of the Jerusalem Church which was led by James, the Lord's brother. The Epistle of James, which may reflect his teaching, seems to fit this pattern. It is firmly in the Jewish tradition. It makes no mention of the Resurrection, but urges its readers to prayer, faith and good works. On the other hand, why should one assume that James's group got Jesus right, while Paul, who clearly did believe that something more had happened, got Jesus wrong?

'We know from the Book of Acts', I insisted, 'that some people who spread the message of Jesus did put great emphasis on the Resurrection and were explicit about the Crucifixion.'

'Yes, of course,' Horsley said. 'Others did focus on the Resurrection, and I would say the most simple explanation here for the emergence of Jesus as the spiritual or religious figure is that it took not just decades but centuries, and our picture becomes an amalgam of what were originally several independent movements.'

I was not convinced. My basic problem with Horsley's interpretation of history was that Jesus became one of the world's greatest spiritual figures, and yet his Jesus seemed to have been leading a political rather than a religious movement. So I suggested to him, 'You seem to be taking the spiritual side right out of Jesus. Do you think that is important?'

Horsley became rather more cautious. 'Perhaps I'm over-emphasizing to get this point across, but what I mean to be saying is that the two can't be separated. Not only can't we separate the religious and political dimensions, we can't separate the spiritual and economic dimensions. This is coming right out of the Hebrew Bible, the Old Testament. What God is really concerned about is that the people have enough to eat.'

The rebel reaches Rome

Jesus was born, preached and died in Palestine, but the Church in Jerusalem was soon eclipsed by the Christian communities outside Palestine. There were a number of reasons for this. The first was persecution. James, the leader of the Jerusalem Church, was beheaded and other Jewish Christians were harassed. The Acts of the Apostles records that members of the Jerusalem Church were scattered. Some ended up in Cyprus and Syria. The spread of Paul's version of Christianity among the Gentiles led to conflict between Jewish and Gentile Christians. But the worst blow to Jewish Christianity was the Jewish War, which began in the year AD 66 and culminated in the destruction of the Temple. The Jews adjusted to the loss by speeding up a process which had been going on for some time: spiritualizing the idea of sacrifice, and refocusing their faith around the home and the synagogue. Jewish Christians, with their fervent belief that the Messiah had come, did not really fit within this new kind of Judaism. Among other Jewish groups which simply disappeared from history after AD 70 were the Sadducees and the Qumran community. On the other hand, outside Palestine Christianity spread into Asia and Egypt, and finally to Rome.

The Roman Church became particularly important, situated as it was in the

OVERLEAF
The dome of St Peter's, Rome. Around the inside
of the dome, below which stands the tomb of Peter, are
Christ's words, 'You are Peter and on this rock
I will build my Church'. The authority of
the Popes is based on the application of
this mandate to Peter's successors.

imperial capital. It was the Roman Empire which provided the roads and the sea links for the earliest missionary voyages, and the *Pax Romana* or Roman peace made these journeys as safe as they could be. The first Christians stayed in touch with one another by letter; doctrines, ideas, arguments and hymns were spread from person to person and church to church along the trade routes of the Roman Empire. As early as the second century Christians saw evidence of the hand of God in the fact that the Emperor Augustus established the *Pax Romana* just at the time Jesus was born. They thought it could not have been a coincidence that the arrangements for spreading the message of Jesus were put in place just at the time they were needed. Even so, life was not always easy for the missionaries. Paul suffered beatings, riots and shipwreck in his attempts to spread the Gospel.

The Roman Empire eventually adopted Christianity as its official religion, with far-reaching consequences for the history of Europe and the rest of the world. So it seemed appropriate for me to go to Rome to see whether I could find any further clues about what I still believed was a miracle, the rapid spread of Christianity after the Crucifixion of its founder.

Standing outside the porch of St Peter's Basilica in Rome, I watched visitors from all over the world filing up the steps: a party of nuns from Japan, or maybe Korea; a bearded American priest wearing the dark brown robes of a Franciscan leading a party, perhaps of his parishioners; a group of young couples stopped by officials for wearing shorts; an Indian family, the wife more adequately covered with a colourful silk sari. It was not the majesty of the vast grey-brown building, but this stream of visitors and pilgrims, which spoke to me of what the Pope's cathedral meant.

Even in our secular century Rome is the capital of a great religious empire which inspires in some devotion, in others like me wonder, and in yet others, I suppose, just curiosity. The Pope no longer rules any territories except the tiny Vatican state, but his spiritual empire has subjects in almost every corner of the world. In my time I have seen the British Empire fade away, the Soviet Empire collapse, and the Shah of Iran, who claimed to be the heir to the Persian Empire, dethroned. But the Pope still has millions of loyal Christian followers who are bound to accept his word as final in matters of faith and doctrine. Yet his empire was founded on defeat, not victory – the defeat of the Crucifixion, and the defeat of the martyrdom of St Peter, the first bishop of Rome, the first Pope. I wondered whether any of those early Christians could possibly have imagined that some two thousand years after their lifetime the monuments of the empire which inflicted such defeats on them – the Forum, the Colosseum, Trajan's markets and many others – would be just tourist sites, while the successor of St Peter ruled in considerable splendour, surrounded by all the treasures that the Vatican had collected down the centuries.

The last verse of one of the best-known evening hymns is:

So be it Lord; thy throne shall never,
Like Earth's proud Empires pass away,
Thy Kingdom stands and grows for ever,
Till all thy creatures own thy sway.

Perhaps that is an exaggeration, and the Church's kingdom will never extend that far. It seems to be contracting now. But it is true to say that, while earthly emperors and empires do pass away, all the founders of great religions – Mohammed, Buddha, Moses and Jesus – do still hold their sway. Religions have shown more staying power than any empire based on earthly might.

The early converts

But if Jesus was a Jewish teacher, or an eschatological prophet, or even a rebel, what made him different from the other rabbis, prophets or rebels of his time? Why did only *his* life and teaching lead to the foundation of a new religion which has survived alongside the other great religions of the world?

First we have to see who the converts to Christianity were. There is no doubt that most of the early Jewish Christians regarded their links with the Law and the prophets as fundamental to their faith. Few of them could read the original Hebrew scriptures, but they did have a Greek version which had been translated for the many Greek-speaking Jews who lived in the cities of the Roman Empire. It took nearly two centuries for Christians from a Jewish background to see themselves as belonging to a different religion. They were in a very real sense still Jews. That is why the writers of the Gospels went to such lengths to demonstrate that Jesus was the fulfilment of the promises that they believed God had made to the children of Israel. The long list of Jesus's forefathers in the very first chapter of St Matthew's Gospel is just one example. That Gospel starts with the words, 'The book of the generation of

Jesus Christ, the son of David, the son of Abraham.' The Church's greatest success, however, was not among Jews, but among the Gentiles or non-Jews.

When St Paul started his missionary journeys in Asia, the obvious groups for him to target were the considerable number of Gentiles who were taking an interest in Judaism. They are described in the Acts of the Apostles as 'those who feared God', and were attracted to the Jewish communities which flourished in many parts of the Empire. In the capital, Rome, there were perhaps as many as eleven synagogues. The Gentiles who were attracted to Judaism found paganism morally and spiritually unsatisfactory. The Roman gods provided a kind of civic religion which supported the status quo, but did not really speak to the soul. Many people were also put off by the erotic and fanciful myths and legends of the gods. Thoughtful people turned to philosophy. There were a number of schools on offer. In Judaism they found monotheism, or belief in one God, which must have seemed to many a more advanced form of religion, more coherent, more rational, and what is more, it had a moral code.

But why then did those interested Gentiles not go the whole way and opt for Judaism? Ed Sanders suggested that if the 'God-fearing' Gentiles *had* become Jews, then Judaism rather than Christianity might have been the monotheistic religion which eventually replaced polytheistic paganism. But this did not happen. One obvious explanation is that the men among the interested Gentiles did not want to be circumcised, which would have been a painful, even dangerous, operation for an adult. As Gentile Christians they did not have to go through this ordeal. St Paul won that battle for them. If they had become Jews they would also have had to keep the strict Jewish food laws, and that would not have been easy for Gentile families from a different cultural background. Ed Sanders said to me that he thought Judaism could never quite change from being a national and ethnic religion. Although there were some Gentile converts to Judaism, it could never have mass appeal for those not born to it.

By becoming Christians, Gentiles got the monotheism and morality of Judaism without its narrower side. They might also have been attracted by something in the new religion which they did not find in Judaism, the stories of Jesus. St Paul laid great stress on Jesus, as Ed Sanders has written in his book on that great missionary, 'He preached the death, resurrection, and lordship of Jesus, and he proclaimed that faith in him guaranteed a share in his life.' The history of all religions shows that there have always been people who have felt the need for a personal relationship with a divine figure, someone to listen to their prayers and understand their hopes and dreads. There must have been Gentiles who found that they could regard Jesus as a friend who had lived a human life like them, and now looked after them from his throne in Heaven. For those without the instinct of faith this may seem strange, incredible even. How can you have a heavenly friend whom you cannot talk with, cannot see, do not even know for certain exists? But it is possible, or at least those with faith find it possible. Looking at an index of the first line of hymns shows that, as do these verses from one of them:

Jesu, these eyes have never seen,
That radiant form of thine;
The veil of sense hangs dark between
Thy blessed face and mine.

I see thee not, I hear thee not,
Yet thou art oft with me;
And earth has ne'er so dear a spot
As where I meet with thee.

Yet though I have not seen, and still
Must rest in faith alone,
I love thee, dearest Lord, and will,
Unseen, but not unknown.

Gentiles may also have been attracted by the Christian emphasis on practical caring. The earliest Christian communities went out of their way to look after outcasts and widows; they also practised healing and exorcisms. One of the great problems in the ancient world was making sure that you had a decent funeral. There were many dining clubs whose members promised to contribute towards a common burial fund and turn out for each other's last rites. To outsiders the early Christian groups would have looked like one of these clubs, the only difference being that its membership was open to all classes of society.

In that famous thirteenth chapter of the First Epistle to the Corinthians St Paul wrote, 'If I have prophetic powers, and understand all mysteries and all knowledge, and if I have all faith . . . if I give away all I have, and if I deliver my body to be burned, but have not love, I gain nothing.' In other words no matter how learned you are, no matter how talented, no matter how law-abiding, no matter how charitable in the sense we understand the word nowadays, you will get nowhere without love. 'Love is patient and kind; love is not jealous or boastful; it is not arrogant or rude. Love does not insist on its own way; it is not irritable or resentful; it does not rejoice at wrong, but rejoices in the right. Love bears all things, believes all things, hopes all things, endures all things.'

The early Christians set an example in their personal relationships that pagans found impressive. They did not always live up to their ideals, as we know from St Paul's Epistles. There were, for instance, the Christians in Corinth to whom he wrote saying, 'It is reported commonly that there is fornication among you.' There were unseemly rows within churches which St Paul complained about too. But there were striking examples of courage, when Christians showed that they could face death without flinching, as exemplified by Stephen, the first martyr, and many martyrs after him – so many that Tertullian is credited with that famous phrase 'The blood of the martyrs is the seed of the Church.' What he actually said, apparently, was, 'The more you mow us down, the more we grow, the seed is the blood of Christians.' The thought, though, is the same, and who would want to lose that famous phrase? Tertullian, who lived from the middle of the second century through into the third, was converted from paganism and became a skilled advocate of the Church's faith.

After the Resurrection

In the vast square outside St Peter's, where pilgrims assemble to hear the Pope speak and to receive his blessing, there stands a tall obelisk. I was told that it had originally stood in the Circus Maximus on the spot where St Peter had been crucified upside down before a hostile crowd. It brought me back to that key question: what happened to the disciples after the Resurrection? How had St Peter, who denied Jesus when he stood in the courtyard of Caiaphas's house, developed into the charismatic leader believed to be the first Pope? How had he become so bold that he was prepared to give his life for his faith?

In Rome I met another American scholar who had different views from both Ed Sanders and Richard Horsley on this subject. He was Dominic Crossan, a small, wiry man with grey hair and a sharp, inquiring face. He told me he was the son of an Irish bank manager, who had joined the Roman Catholic Servite order and been sent to America to train to be a monk. He became a biblical scholar too, spending two years at the French Bible School in Jerusalem where Father Jerry still teaches. Eighteen years after joining he left the Servites for two reasons. He wanted to marry, and he wanted to be free from what he has described as 'the irritation of having been trained to think critically but being in constant trouble for doing it'. Since then he has been teaching at De Paul University in Chicago which, although a Roman Catholic university, was prepared to accept a former priest into the theology department. He has written a book on Jesus which is sub-titled *A Revolutionary Biography*, and is now working on a book which aims to get behind the Acts of the Apostles and discover the historical earliest Church. Who better, then, to discuss with me the transformation of the followers of Jesus into the Church?

Dominic Crossan is widely read in several academic disciplines and applies what he learns from all of them to his study of the life of Jesus. Like Richard Horsley, he believes it is important to look at the social sciences and what they tell us about peasant societies as well as examining archaeology and studying the biblical texts. So I was not surprised that he suggested we should use early Christian art to illustrate his view of Jesus's life and the birth of the Church. We went to the church of SS Nereo ed Achilleo which stands above the largest catacomb in Rome. As we waited for the catacombs to be opened we watched two elderly nuns sweeping the paths of the garden in which we were sitting. I thought, 'They have the simple faith which doesn't question the Resurrection, doesn't ask how the Church was born and how it grew. They accept Jesus as God and the Church as the hand-maid of God. It's strange that Christian historians like Dominic Crossan now seem to be undermining that faith.'

Eventually the gates were opened and we went down into underground passages known as the catacombs. There were several hundred miles of these passages in ancient Rome, and many of them ran under the main roads leading out of the city because the law did not permit burial within the city walls: it was believed that the bodies cause pollution. As we walked along one of the passages Dominic Crossan explained to me that it was the ordinary people of Rome who were buried there. The élite buried their dead in mausolea, at ground level. Sometimes the passages were dug one under the other, as many as four storeys deep. In the walls of the passage through which we were walking niches had been cut, into which the bodies had been placed. Dominic Crossan pointed out some very narrow niches, explaining that they were where children had been buried.

'The others don't look exactly large,' I said.

'Very few people were really tall,' Dominic replied. 'You're talking about people not much above five feet.'

'Many of them would have died very young, too?'

'Well, I think about a third of the population would have gone by the age

The bread and fish meals of the Gospels (ABOVE) lie behind
the Christian Eucharist. The significance of this painting, in
the catacomb of Priscilla in Rome, is that the dead
are feasting with the living, their communion unbroken.
The veiled figure, third from the right, may well be
the deceased, and the figure on the left, a bishop.

The Good Shepherd (RIGHT), the earliest attempt to portray
Jesus, painted on the ceiling of a small chapel in the catacomb
of Priscilla. The motif was popular among the Roman Christians
as the shepherd was a familiar figure of the classical
mythology they shared with their pagan neighbours.

of six and maybe another third by the age of sixteen. The life expectancy was about twenty-eight for males and twenty-six or twenty-seven for females.'

I had been brought up on stories of Christians hiding from persecution in these dark passages. But Dominic Crossan dismissed that as nonsense, pointing out that the Roman authorities knew perfectly well where the catacombs were.

We entered a small chamber with pictures painted on the wall and the ceiling. These stucco paintings were the earliest known examples of Christian art. But I noticed there were no pictures of the scenes that a visitor to any church would see, or indeed anyone who had read St Paul's epistles would expect to see. There was no Crucifixion, no Resurrection, no Jesus in triumph. There was a picture of Jesus as a shepherd carrying a ram, one of Jesus performing a healing miracle, and another of Jesus as a baby in his mother's arms. The lack of any pictures of the Crucifixion or the Resurrection did, I suppose, add force to Dominic Crossan's sceptical argument about the Resurrection. He did not believe that the emergence of the Church needed a miraculous resurrection to explain it. In one of his books he had written, 'It is a terrible trivialization to imagine that all Jesus's followers lost their faith on Good Friday and had it restored by apparitions on Easter Sunday. It is another trivialization to presume that even those who lost their nerve, fled and hid, lost their faith, hope and love.' Dominic Crossan maintained, 'Easter is not about the start of a new faith, but about the continuation of an old one.'

The healing ministry continues

As I found the disciples' reported belief that Jesus was risen the most satisfactory explanation for the birth of the Church, I was interested to learn what alternative Dominic Crossan could put forward. So I asked him, 'How do you believe the Jesus movement survived the Crucifixion?'

He had a simple but convincing answer. 'Because the followers kept healing. Because there were people in Galilee who went on healing probably for a month before they even found out Jesus was dead. The Kingdom of God didn't stop at three o'clock on that Friday afternoon. It still went on. They were still experiencing the power of God through Jesus, and Jesus was God. So somehow they found Jesus was still present.'

'What about those who say that the disciples lost their faith and only regained it because something truly remarkable called the Resurrection happened?'

'That's the way the story has been told in the last chapters of the Gospels. It's the official version. But I don't think it's necessarily right. I think the followers of Jesus lost their nerve, not their faith. They ran, and maybe that was a very good thing, but losing your nerve is a very different thing from losing your faith. They didn't lose their faith. I think that would be a libel on the first Christians.'

'So do you think nothing like the Resurrection happened?'

'Well, there were visions, of course. We know Paul had a vision. Visions happen at the start of every religious movement, so I think visions can be taken for granted. But visions are always of what you most want or desperately fear. They don't explain why you have that want, that love, or that fear. That comes from the movement that was there before Jesus. So the Resurrection for me means the continuation of that movement. Someone listening to Paul can experience the power of God through Jesus. He doesn't then say, "I believe you, Paul," but "I believe God. I can experience this empowerment."' Dominic Crossan lays great stress on the fact that Jesus empowered his followers. He insists that Jesus did not retain a monopoly on his power of healing. He sent his followers out to heal too.

The Acts of the Apostles shows that healing miracles continued in the early Church. St Peter and St John healed a lame man who was begging for alms outside the temple. St Peter is reported to have brought a woman called Tabitha back to life. I also particularly like the story in Acts about the woman who was able to divine the future and made a lot of money for her masters by 'soothsaying'. She made a nuisance of herself to Paul and his colleagues by following them everywhere. Paul eventually said to the spirit in her, 'I charge you in the name of Jesus Christ to come out of her.' The spirit did come out of her, much to the annoyance of her masters. They took Paul and his companion Silas before the magistrates, who had them beaten and sent to jail.

St Paul obviously believed he had been empowered, and also believed he could empower others. For instance, in Corinth when he laid hands on new converts, 'The Holy Spirit came on them; and they spoke with tongues and prophesied.' St Paul believed in the power of visions, too: he was converted by a vision. According to the Acts of the Apostles it was also a vision which convinced St Peter that he must break with his prejudices against Gentiles, and not call anyone 'common or unclean'. To his astonishment the gift of the Holy Spirit was poured out on a Roman centurion and his household. This vision was crucial to the future of the Church. If Peter had not accepted the Gentiles, the split between Jewish and Gentile converts might have been unbridgeable. Given the importance of visions in the early years of the Church, I can see that it is possible that the sightings of Jesus which led to the belief in the Resurrection could also have been visions.

But I was still confused by the pictures on the walls of the catacombs. St Paul might have been convinced that the power of Jesus lived on because of the miracles that he was able to perform in his name, but he was also convinced of the importance of the Crucifixion and Resurrection. Jesus's victory over death was an essential part of his teaching and dominates his letters to the churches. So why did the early Christians not paint pictures on these themes? Should there not also be a picture of the Last Judgement? Death, the hope of Resurrection and concern about judgement would surely be the subjects on the minds of Christians at the time they were burying their dead. So I asked Dominic Crossan, 'Are you suggesting that because there are no pictures of the Crucifixion and the Resurrection they were not important to the early Christians?'

'No,' he replied firmly, 'I wouldn't want to say that, and wouldn't want to say there was a complete disjunction between popular piety and the official, scribal piety that we read in the Gospel texts, but if you ask, "What was on people's minds", the answer is that they saw Jesus as a deliverer from the pain of life's agonies. It's the healing stories rather than simply the raising from the dead that seem to impress them.'

Dominic Crossan believed that the early artists' concern with Jesus's healing and Jesus at the table was an accurate representation of his life's work too. From his book I knew that he, like Richard Horsley, saw Jesus as a rebel, and placed great importance on the economic circumstances of Galilee at the time, with the Roman cities draining the economy and the peasants getting into debt and losing their land.

When I asked him how he saw the life of the rebel Jesus in the pictures on the walls and the ceiling of the chamber we were in, he said, 'Two things are very important to me, the eating and the healing. That goes back to Jesus, and both are demonstrated here.' Pointing to a picture of the raising of Lazarus he went on, 'That's the scene of Jesus's healing which appears most frequently

This peasant Jesus shows the popularity of liberation theology
among the poor of Latin America. Since the 1960s it has
been a tenet of much of the Church's social teaching that God has
chosen the poor and wills social justice. This has put
new emphasis on the political implications of Jesus's teaching.
Fernando Botero, *Head of Christ*, 1964.

in Christian art before the Emperor Constantine adopted Christianity as the official religion.' Then, pointing in another direction, he said, 'Over there you can see the bottom half of a man carrying his bed. The paralytic has been healed. That's the second most frequent scene after Lazarus in Christian art before Constantine.'

Looking at the heavy bed the paralytic was carrying in the painting, I said, 'The poor man would have got ill all over again carrying that.'

Dominic Crossan laughed. 'I think he'd end up in a Roman hospital if he carried a bed like that. Maybe that's what paralysed him in the first place. In reality he would have had a sort of rolled up mat, and to take up his bed and walk would have been very easy. Visualize it as a Roman would, and you end up with this heavy iron bedstead. Now look over here,' Dominic Crossan went on. 'You have a meal scene. A group of people sitting round a table. Now look up at the ceiling. You have a shepherd. It's a young, beardless, healing God. You don't have an old, bearded God, but a new healer. That's how the early Christians saw Jesus.'

'Why are healing and feeding so important? How do you join them together?'

'Well, in the earliest material about Jesus, say in St Mark's Gospel, Jesus sends people out. He tells them they are to heal and to eat with the people they heal. The mission of Jesus is directed at the peasants who have been pushed off their lands, pushed from poverty into destitution. For them, healing and eating are the core problems.'

'Because they don't get enough to eat?'

'Because first of all they don't get enough to eat. It's as basic as that. That's why the first thing Jesus talks about in the Our Father is enough bread for today. We won't even look for tomorrow, just enough bread for today. That's what destitute people need.'

'And the healing?'

'Jesus sends out travelling healers to the householders. Now why do the householders need healing? The answer is that these are the people who are terrified. They're terrified of being pushed off their land, pushed into destitution and losing their land. So Jesus is creating an interaction between the poor and the destitute. I think that's the group Jesus is especially working with, people who are between poverty and destitution.'

Dominic Crossan also believed with Richard Horsley that Jesus was trying to reconstitute Galilean peasant society so that they could support each other, stand together. He, like Horsley, thought Jesus himself might have slipped from poverty into destitution.

That, I still felt, was unlikely because history does not record many examples of the destitute throwing up great leaders. Dominic agreed. But he also said, 'He was not founding a kingdom of beggars, but a movement in which the newly destitute and those who were terrified they would soon be destitute were standing together.'

There are some scholars who believe that the real point of the stories about Jesus eating and healing with social outcasts is to demonstrate his opposition to the strict rules of purity imposed by Jewish law. But Dominic did not agree. 'I don't put nearly as much emphasis on that as some scholars have. I think Jesus was a peasant. I wish those scholars would ask the simple question, "How did the day labourer in Galilee observe kosher?" Think of him working thirty, forty or fifty days a year. If he worked for a pagan for a day and he got a meal as part of his fee would he really ask questions about the purity laws, or would he just take what food he could get? And if he did, does that mean he is un-Orthodox or not a good Jew?'

It was a good point, but my experience in India had taught me how all-pervasive purity laws can be, so I pointed out, 'Peasants in India do observe laws of caste. They eat with some people and they don't eat with others. It is the dispossessed, the people Jesus was concentrating on, who suffer from purity rules, and there are some scholars who compare the dispossessed in Galilee of Jesus's time with the untouchables of India.'

Dominic thought those scholars were not being historical. 'What we have to do is ask what was law observance like in the first twenty years of the first century in the Jewish homeland. We're not talking about two hundred years later, when the religion of the rabbis and the Pharisees had become the norm in Judaism. By that time the Temple was gone and Judaism had to survive by turning every home into a miniature purified Temple. The rabbis had to impose strict purity to prevent Judaism from being totally destroyed. All of that is perfectly understandable after the destruction of the Temple. But it doesn't tell us about what Jewish law observance meant in the first century and what it meant across the social classes. The caste system was not there yet.'

My biggest problem with seeing Jesus as a social revolutionary has always

ADLOCVTIO
QVADIVINI
TVS IMPVLSI
CONSTANTINI
ANI VICTORIAM
REPERERE

Constantine ascribed his victory at the battle
of the Milvian Bridge in AD 312 to a vision
of the Cross, emblazoned (in Greek) with
the words, 'In this sign, conquer'.
School of Raphael, the Vatican,
Rome, sixteenth century.

been that it doesn't seem to leave much room for God. Yet according to the gospels Jesus's whole life and teaching was centred on God. I told Dominic that I did not find God in his picture of Jesus, and suggested he had missed out something rather important.

He replied, 'You want to know what the Kingdom of God is? It's the will of God "on Earth as in Heaven". Heaven's in great shape, Heaven's in beautiful shape, it's the Earth that's a mess. What God wills for Earth is the Kingdom of God. The God of Jesus is really a God of radical justice, very profoundly radical justice. Now whether that is still the God of Christians is something each Christian has to answer in his or her own heart.'

Dominic's answer reminded me of the Catholic priests who had developed liberation theology, concentrating on the God of radical justice. They had been criticized by the Church and told that they were Marxists. While I strongly support liberation theology's concern for the poor and the view that there is something fundamentally wrong with the global economy which lays so much stress on creating wealth and so little on how it is created or distributed, I have always been worried by those who lay such stress on the economic side of Christianity that the spiritual seems to get forgotten. The evidence that Jesus was deeply concerned about economic reforms is questionable. Ed Sanders has written, 'Jesus the social and economic planner simply cannot be found in the gospels.' If Jesus had been a radical economist, why had the early Church not been radical too? Although it is reported in the Acts of the Apostles that the Jerusalem Church did experiment with a form of common ownership, most of the evidence points to an organization which sought an accommodation with the Roman Empire, especially after the Christians separated from the Jews. But when I put that point to Dominic he had an explanation.

'One thing which happened, of course, was that the movement moved out

The Majesty of Christ, late thirteenth-century mosaic
in the church of Hagia Sophia, Constantinople.
This was the pre-eminent church of Christendom in
the Byzantine Empire; the emperor's earthly rule was
subordinate only to the cosmic rule of Christ.
Under Islamic rule the church became a mosque
and it is now a museum.

of the countryside into the city. You have to try to calculate the gains and losses of that. You could say, "well, there goes everything." Would it have been better if the Jesus movement had died out in the pristine purity of Galilee? Well, maybe, but it didn't. It moved into the cities, and the social class of converts started getting a little higher.' According to Dominic the Christians in the city were still concerned about social justice, but no longer only for the poorest of the poor. Urban Christianity spread among 'free' men and women. They were the people who had managed to buy their way out of slavery.

As the years passed, the Church appears to have become less and less concerned with social and economic matters. It concerned itself with forming a Christian moral code, defending itself against criticisms from Jews and pagans, and building the community structures which enabled it to survive. There were times when Christians were persecuted, but the Church continued to expand. It was so successful, in terms of increasing its numbers and its influence, that within three hundred years of Jesus's death the Emperor Constantine decided to adopt Christianity as a recognized religion under imperial patronage.

The conversion of Constantine

The details of Constantine's conversion are not clear. He came to power at a time when the Empire was torn apart by internal conflicts. He himself had to fight for supremacy against a powerful rival. According to tradition he became convinced that he was favoured by the Christian God when he had a vision at the crucial battle of the Milvian Bridge in AD 312. He saw a cross in the sky inscribed with the phrase 'In this sign you conquer' in Latin. After that battle Constantine changed the imperial arms to a design based on the Greek letters *chi* and *rho*, the first two letters of 'Christ'. He supported a huge construction programme throughout the Empire to build churches in every city alongside, and eventually replacing, the temples of the pagan gods. Constantine was not baptized until he was on his deathbed, although that was not uncommon because at that time the penances required of someone who sinned after baptism were extremely severe.

Constantine need not have chosen Christianity. There were alternatives available – popular religions from Persia, Syria and Egypt. When Constantine was already a junior partner in the Imperial Government the Emperor Diocletian declared Mithras, the god of a Persian religion, protector of the Empire. The historian Hugh Trevor-Roper has written, 'From that moment Mithraism might have become the religion of Rome. Had it done so . . . the baptism with bull's blood in underground caves would have replaced the crucifixion and the sacrament of the last supper at the centre of European worship.'

It is not easy to judge how far Constantine was sincere in his Christian faith. What is clear is that he recognized Christianity as the only moral and spiritual force which could bind the fragmented Empire together and give it a new impetus. Christianity was by then the most successful religion, and what must have particularly attracted Constantine was the way the faith had spread in the countryside. The rural areas provided the soldiers of the imperial army and had by then become more important to the emperor than the cities.

Constantine took a keen interest in the affairs of the Church, wanting to ensure that it remained an effective force for unity. He tried to resolve controversies, and once described himself as 'the bishop of external things'. As emperor he helped pass judgement on those Christians who had compromised with the authorities during the persecution of the previous century, after a commission of bishops and a synod had failed to resolve the issue. He also summoned the historic Council of Nicaea to settle a long-running controversy over the status of Jesus: was he fully divine or not? Constantine's decision to opt for Christianity made him, in the view of Hugh Trevor-Roper, 'The man who perhaps exercised the greatest influence on the history of the west than any man since Christ.'

Christianity and the Eastern Empire

So if Dominic Crossan is right, the rebel Jesus became the patron of the empire he had rebelled against. To discover the difference that this made to Jesus and the Church, I went with Dominic to Ravenna in Italy to see the magnificent mosaics.

Ravenna is on the Adriatic, the Eastern coast, of Italy. It became a centre of evangelism under its first bishop Apollinaris in the second century. After the conversion of Constantine, it was an important city with its own cathedral, baptistery and bishop's residence. In the late fifth century Ravenna

became the capital of the Gothic 'Kings of Italy' who had overcome the Western Roman Emperors. Some important buildings including churches were continued under the Ostrogothic King Theodoric in the early sixth century. Some of its most magnificent churches were decorated after the army of the Eastern Emperor Justinian occupied the city in AD 540. Justinian was determined to make it clear that he had responsibility for matters spiritual as well as temporal. He saw it as his responsibility to guard the Church as well as guide the state. In his zeal to promote Christianity Justinian persecuted those whom he regarded as heretics, and forced many pagans to be baptized.

One of the finest churches in Ravenna is the basilica of San Vitale. When I approached the pale pink building with Dominic it was glowing in the sunlight. I was reminded of the pink Indian sandstone, so familiar to me from the Presidential Palace and the Secretariat at the heart of New Delhi. This church, however, was built of wafer-thin bricks held in place by layers of lime of the same width. It was eight-sided, surmounted by a stubby octagonal tower with a cross on the top. At the east end there was a semi-circular extension, or apse. Separate and higher than the church's tower stood a cylindrical belltower, capped by a dome.

Inside the church eight pillars supported the dome, which I had not seen from outside because it was covered by the tower. In the centre of the dome there was a white paschal lamb set against a dark blue background studded with white and golden stars and surrounded by a wreath of leaves. The wreath enclosing the lamb was held aloft by four white-robed angels who merged into a green and golden background of leaves populated by animals and birds. In one corner there were four peacocks with magnificent tails spread like fans. The peacock is a symbol of the Resurrection. This was certainly the lamb on high, Christ in Heaven, not the earthly good shepherd of the catacombs.

We walked up to the semi-circular apse at the east end of the church. There I saw a very regal Jesus. He was dressed in an imperial purple robe and sat on a blue globe, signifying creation. He held the roll with the seven seals of the Book of Revelation in one hand and in the other a crown which he was giving to the martyr St Vitalis. There were angels on both sides of Jesus. The Bishop of Ravenna held in his hand the eight-sided church, offering it to Jesus. On the left side of the apse, well below Jesus, was a mosaic of the Emperor Justinian surrounded by imperial courtiers, soldiers and Church dignitaries.

The two mosaics seemed to signify Jesus co-opted by the Empire, part of the panoply of imperial splendour, designed to impress, perhaps even oppress, the subject people whom Justinian had reconquered. But when I suggested this to Dominic he did not fully agree.

'Well, your first impression would be that the Emperor is there, clothed in purple,' he said, 'and he has a halo round his head. But notice two things. He is carrying a gift, which is rather large and gold. He's taking it towards Jesus. Notice also he's standing up. Now when you turn from the Emperor to the mosaic of Jesus your eyes are lifted higher. You can see that Jesus is seated, not standing. He's on a throne and the throne is the world, and the only people up there with him besides the angels are a martyr and the bishop. There are no imperial courtiers up there.' He went on, 'The important thing is that Jesus seated on the world is still just wearing sandals, like the sandals of the Jesus who started it all, long, long ago in the hills of Galilee.'

So this imperial Jesus had not just been co-opted by the emperor, he had conquered him. The rebel who was executed by one Roman emperor now sat on high while another emperor stood below bearing a gift. Yet he remained the same rebel, the leader of the emperor's poorest and most despised subjects.

Supremacy over the emperor was not won easily. Dominic thinks that it was finally gained by the settlement of the Arian controversy, which I had always been taught to think was a purely doctrinal matter about the precise definition of Jesus's divinity. Dominic saw a political dimension here too. The Arian controversy was a long battle between the followers of Arius, who believed that Jesus was a semi-divine being, a kind of godlet, and Orthodox believers who claimed he was fully divine, equal with God, as well as being human. According to Dominic, much more was at stake than just theology. If Jesus was less than fully divine, then the Emperor could claim to be his equal. After all, emperors were traditionally thought to have almost god-like status. But if Jesus was fully divine he would always be superior to the emperor. It is interesting that Constantine at first backed the orthodox view and played an important role in the Council at Nicaea which decided the debate in favour of orthodoxy. Later, however, he seems to have had second thoughts, perhaps when he realized that bishops could appeal to the divine Jesus above his head.

The mosaics at Ravenna do not represent a final victory for Jesus and the Church over the state. The battle was fought again and again. It was fought by medieval popes, it was won by Archbishop Thomas à Becket when he resisted the power of Henry II. It was, perhaps, lost for a time when Henry VIII broke with the papacy. In Germany during the Second World War some Christians regarded it as their prime duty to be loyal to the state, while others believed that loyalty to Jesus came first. They disobeyed Hitler's Government, sometimes facing terrible consequences.

But the victory that the Church scored over the emperors was crucial. If the emperors had succeeded in subduing the Church, its mission would have been blunted and it would probably have become just the branch of the administration responsible for religion. Perhaps the emperor rather than the pope might have been known as Pontifex Maximus, the supreme pontiff.

Whenever the Church has been linked to the state there have been some clerics who have succumbed to the temptations of power, prestige and wealth. But equally there have always been Christians who have refused to compromise with the state. It was because of those who were determined that the state should not swamp the Church that Jesus could wear the purple robe but still retain his sandals. When Christianity spread with imperialism again – the imperialism of Portugal, Spain, Britain and other European nations – there were missionaries who refused to be co-opted to the cause of their governments at home. That's why in countries like India there were Christians who chose the option for the poor long before it was brought into prominence by liberation theology.

What of the divine Jesus?

After my travels with Richard Horsley and Dominic Crossan I understood how Jesus could be interpreted as a rebel, and how valuable his identification with the poor had been for Christianity. But this still left me wondering what had happened to Jesus the divine, the Christ I had been brought up to worship. It seemed to me the two scholars had ripped away so much traditional teaching that there was nothing left of the divine Jesus. Perhaps it was wrong to describe their portrait as Christian at all.

On my last evening in Ravenna I had dinner with Dominic and his wife Sarah. I felt I had to raise this problem, so I asked him what I was soon to realize was a very naive question. 'It seems to me that you can't still be a Roman Catholic holding the views about Jesus you now do. Am I right?'

He smiled and said, 'No, actually you're not, although I understand your problem. Many people have told me that having left the priesthood and the life of a monk I must be against the Church, against monasticism and against dogma. They say that at best I must be seeking an excuse for leaving them, and at worst I'm taking revenge.'

Certainly Dominic didn't strike me as a man consumed by anger because he thought he had wasted years as a priest and a monk. He was clearly a remarkably balanced man, someone at peace with himself, and I could well believe him when he said, 'While I was a priest and a religious I was quite happy. I am grateful for my education in the seminary. I still love the Georgian chants which I sang very badly for three or four hours in daily choir. And I'm grateful for what I learnt of the Bible alongside the study of philosophy, theology and canon law – all of which I found arid. When I wasn't happy in the order I left, and I have been very happy since.' He said he still regarded himself not just as a Christian, but as a Christian with a special duty. He felt he had a responsibility to free Christianity from a literal interpretation of the New Testament. A good dinner in an Italian restaurant can be distracting, and so I asked him whether he had ever written anything which explained his position. He agreed to send me an article he had written called 'Almost the Whole Truth'.

It contained what I take to be his personal creed.

> The last chapters of the gospels and the first chapter of Acts taken literally, factually and historically trivialize Christianity and brutalize Judaism. That acceptation has created in Christianity a lethal deceit that sours its soul, hardens its heart, and savages its spirit. . . . I never presume that we find the historical Jesus once and for all and I never separate the historical Jesus from the Christ of faith. Jesus Christ is the combination of a fact (Jesus) and an interpretation (Christ). They should neither be separated or confused, and each must be found anew in every generation for their structural dialectic is the heart of Christianity.

I have thought long and hard about those words. I understand that our knowledge is expanding particularly fast in this generation, and that any interpretation of the historical Jesus must be able to stand up to the scrutiny of not just theologians but also historians, linguists, sociologists, anthropologists and economists. I can also see that a Jesus too tightly wrapped in unchanging dogma is an easy target for sceptics using the knowledge now available. I appreciate the damage that those Christians who have stuck doggedly to their traditions have done. They have made Christianity unacceptable to those who cannot believe in all their teachings. But I still find it difficult to accept that the first Christians would have believed that Jesus the rebel was a unique manifestation of God, and if they did not believe that, I do not understand how the Church and its teaching came about.

4

The Hidden Jesus

The Search for a Personal Leader

As an undergraduate I was attracted to the Roman Catholic Church. From the outside it seemed united, universal, disciplined and directed. In contrast, the Anglican Church, into which I was confirmed, seemed divided, undisciplined and anything but universal. Even in England, where it was 'by law established', it often failed to reach those with whom Jesus was most concerned – the poor and the marginalized. Anglicanism seemed to be a religion strictly for the middle classes. I admired the way that the Roman Catholic Church embraced all sections of British society, from the Duke of Norfolk to immigrant Irish workers, and it was impressive that so many stayed faithful. In those days you knew that anywhere in the world you went to church you would get the same Latin mass, but that was not true of Anglican churches. Even in England you could never be quite sure what to expect. Although the clergy were legally obliged to use the words of the Book of Common Prayer, those words could be used for a high mass celebrated with splendour that went as far as, and even beyond, the ceremonial of the Roman Catholics. On the other hand it might be a straight service of Holy Communion, like the ones I was used to from school. Or it could be evangelical worship with spontaneous ad hoc prayers, which I found embarrassing.

What attracted me most was that the Roman Catholic Church told you what to believe, and what the rules were. You knew you had to go to mass every Sunday. Confession was mandatory before communion. You ate fish on Friday. I was attracted by a Church which would do my thinking for me. The Anglican Church was à la carte: you could choose your menu, what you believed, and what rules you kept. I didn't want to leave my own Church, and so I did the next best thing to becoming Roman Catholic: I put myself in the hands of an Anglican priest and let him do my thinking for me. In later life I came to realize that was just what was wrong with me. I wanted to be told what to do; I did not have the courage to find out for myself. So, outside the confines of university, and away from my guardian priest, my ecclesiastical Jesus started to disappear. My church-going declined, my concern with my sins withered away, and eventually it was difficult for me to regard myself as within the Church at all, although I could never bring myself to admit as much.

The Church as an institution is a problem for many people, as it was for me. At its worst it can crush legitimate inquiry and cramp people's spiritual life. There is often such a concentration on rules that all the freshness goes out of religion. I still believe that, without the Church, Jesus would not have survived as the powerful figure he still is today. I like to see the Church as a lampshade which prevents the light of the faith being blown out, and which perhaps protects us from too intense an encounter with spiritual realities. But the history of the Church shows how often the shade dims the light of those with fresh insights about God, or even old insights which have been lost and need reviving. Sometimes it does its utmost to prevent their light being seen at all.

The powerful medieval Church, which was a huge landowner all over Europe, tried to repress the Franciscan order when its members began preaching poverty and an itinerant lifestyle. St Francis of Assisi was right to think that his vision of Christianity was much more in harmony with the life of Jesus than the comfortable wealth of abbots and princes: but the Church had so dimmed the light of Jesus's teaching that it tried to stamp out the Franciscans as heretics. The Franciscans not only survived, but flourished, until they became a powerful, established order in their own right.

After the Reformation another radical teacher had difficulties with the Church. Ignatius of Loyola developed a way of prayer based on a personal relationship with the Jesus of the Gospels. This encouraged people, as Margaret Hebblethwaite has said in her book *Finding God in All Things*, 'to proceed at their own speed, as God led each individual'. To his Catholic critics this sounded far too like the Protestant individualism that the Church had condemned. Ignatius ran foul of the Spanish Inquisition and had to go to Paris to complete his studies. The ecclesiastical authorities accused his followers, the Jesuits, of being seduced by private mystical experiences and told them that they should allow the Church to decide the way to Jesus. The Jesuits, like the Franciscans, won over their critics and increased in numbers and influence to become one of the most effective missionary orders that the Church has ever known. As a mark of their loyalty to the Church, they made a special point of obedience to the Pope. The Jesuits became known as formidable guardians of Catholic orthodoxy, even playing a part in the Inquisition. In more recent years they have become radical again, speaking up powerfully for the poor and oppressed. In reaction, the cautious instincts of the Church are running true to form again, because the conservative members of the Church hierarchy disapprove of liberation theology and are attempting to dim the new light that the Jesuits, and others, are shedding.

The Wesley brothers were devout members of the Church of England, who saw how dimly the light of faith shone in eighteenth-century England. The established Church seemed to have nothing to say to the mass of workers who were moving from the land to the new industries: it preached a dry, rational religion of good behaviour and social conformity. John Wesley was gripped by the message of the Gospel to transform lives. He was no social radical, but he did believe that every individual was capable of experiencing the love of God. He travelled eight thousand miles on horseback to bring his message to the people; but he was seen, not as an asset to the Church, but as a dangerous enthusiast. After his death his followers broke away from the Church of England. Thus the Methodist Church was founded, with its intense stress on personal holiness and the wonderful hymns of John's brother, Charles.

These three examples from Church history show that the institution has difficulty with those who inspire, who throw fresh light, rather than just teach. In particular it has always had difficulty with those who offer the possibility of direct spiritual experience to individuals.

But it is inspiration that people are searching for now. It is surely significant that the branches of the Church which are growing are those that seem to offer a profound and personal experience of Jesus. Evangelicalism is on the increase, with its emphasis on a one-to-one relationship with Christ. There is also now a great revival of interest in the spiritual exercises of St Ignatius. The Jesus whom many Christians are looking for today is a personal Lord who can lead each of us on our individual way to God. Such a Jesus is a sage, a guru, a teacher of wisdom. The problem with the personal Jesus, from the

Church's point of view, is that he has often inspired his followers to be critical of religious authorities. They tend to argue that, just as Jesus was opposed to the religious authorities of his time, so we should be opposed to all who claim too much spiritual authority over the lives of others.

Is there a historical basis for the belief that the original Jesus was such a figure – a critic, an outsider who subverted authority and institutions, even religious ones? There are scholars who argue that there is. They make their case on the basis of the sayings and stories of Jesus, not only the ones found in the four Gospels, but others which were never recognized as canonical and official. There is evidence to suggest that the Church did its best to hide any documents and suppress any sayings which suggested that Jesus might have had difficulties with Christian orthodoxy. There were also some groups of early Christians who openly sought their own Jesus. Some were suspicious of the Jesus of the Church, and others downright hostile to him. This too would indicate that from the start of Christianity there were some who believed that Jesus himself was an outsider.

The influence of Egypt

Egypt was the scene of an early battle between Christian orthodoxy and those who followed alternative traditions about Jesus. Egypt was, of course, the centre of a very ancient civilization. It is a vast museum of the past, an archaeologist's playground. The hot, dry desert climate preserves material which would otherwise have perished: temples and pyramids, papyri and pottery, hieroglyphic writing and mummified bodies. Yet the influence of this civilization on Christianity has largely been ignored by Western scholars. They ignored the geography – Egypt and Palestine are neighbours. Instead, they have concentrated almost entirely on the Jewish and Greek influences on Christian belief and practice. However, according to St Matthew, Jesus spent some of his earliest days in Egypt.

Egyptian civilization had great powers of survival: the dynasty of the Pharaohs lasted for thirty centuries. In the Old Testament it was a Pharaoh who put the Hebrew slave Joseph in charge of the preparations for seven years of famine after he had interpreted the ruler's dream of seven 'sleek' cows followed by seven 'gaunt and thin' cows. Another Pharaoh set cruel task-masters over the Hebrew people and tried to prevent their escape from slavery, in spite of the seven plagues which God sent as punishment. The Pharaohs were eventually conquered by Alexander the Great in 332 BC. Alexander was greeted as their successor, and founded the great city of Alexandria on the Mediterranean coast.

After Alexander's death, generals divided his empire and Ptolemy became the ruler of Egypt; he made Greek the official language and introduced Hellenistic civilization. But he and his successors in the Ptolemaic dynasty allowed Egypt's ancient culture and religion to flourish alongside the new civilization. The Ptolemies also took an interest in Jewish culture and had rabbis translate the Hebrew scriptures into Greek. So the Greek influence on Judaism and Christianity was tempered by Egyptian culture. One of the best-known Egyptian Jews was Philo, a contemporary of Jesus who wrote commentaries on the Jewish scriptures. He interpreted the historical sagas as allegories pointing to timeless truths, and believed that the true God was eternal and transcendent. So when the scriptures said that God appeared to someone – to Moses in the burning bush, for example – he argued that it was the Word of God who appeared. The Word of God was a kind of second God, a communicating God, who could take the form of an angel or messenger. This laid the foundation for Jesus to be seen as God's Word in St John's Gospel. The concept of a second God was also the seed of the doctrine of the Trinity.

By the time that Jesus was born, the last Egyptian queen, Cleopatra, and her Roman lover Mark Antony had been defeated and Egypt was incorporated in the Roman Empire, bringing yet another influence to bear in that ancient country. Into this melting pot of civilizations came Christianity. Tradition claims that it was St Mark who first brought the faith to Egypt. Alexandria, the cultural capital, became an important Christian diocese, with Bible scholars building on Philo's philosophy to explain the significance of Jesus to a pagan world. It is perhaps not surprising that the Church, with its belief that Jesus fulfilled the Hebrew scriptures, did its best to hide the ancient civilization which was still revered among the pagans of Egypt.

It was a sense that the Church had grown soft and had lost the original vigour of Jesus's message which created a rift between orthodoxy and Christians seeking their own Jesus. During the first three centuries of the Christian era there were waves of persecution against the Church, interspersed with periods of relative tolerance. Martyrdom was written into

Christianity from the beginning. After all, Jesus had died for his beliefs; and after him, James, 'the Lord's brother', the leader of the Jerusalem Church, was martyred, and Peter, who, tradition claims, was crucified in Rome. At the end of the third century, when Diocletian was emperor, there was a new outbreak of persecution against Christians.

Stories about martyrs abounded and were highly popular. A Christian monk, Apollonius, was reported to have encouraged many believers in Alexandria to seek martyrdom. Eventually he was brought to trial before a pagan judge. The first thing that the monk said was that he forgave his accusers. One of them was so impressed that he immediately became a Christian, telling the judge that the accusation was unjust. The judge angrily decreed that both Apollonius and his former accuser should be burnt alive. As the fire was lit, the flames were miraculously doused by a cloud of dewy mist. Later Christians were told that the judge and the crowd watching the martyrdom were so amazed that they cried out, 'There is one God, the God of the Christians.' The Roman prefect of Alexandria heard of the incident and sent soldiers to summon Apollonius, the judge and his original accuser into his presence. On the way, Apollonius's testimony converted the soldiers. The result was that they all appeared in chains before the prefect. The situation was getting out of hand and so the prefect hastily ordered them all to be thrown into the sea before Apollonius could convert anyone else.

Whatever the exact detail of Apollonius's trial and death, his story and other reports of martyrdom had an enormous impact. The persecuted Christians were particularly encouraged by accounts of miracles associated with martyrdom. Many actively sought martyrdom as the one death which would guarantee a heavenly reward, the martyr's crown of everlasting life. Their conviction was not unlike that of the young Muslim suicide bombers who die for their faith today, happy in the belief that they have achieved a sure passport to heaven.

The age of the martyrs came to an abrupt end when the Emperor Constantine declared Christianity an official religion. Now, for the first time, the state was on the side of the Church, not persecuting it. It was suddenly fashionable, and socially advantageous, to be a Christian. Inevitably this caused a reaction. What became of the intensity and purity of the faith when it was tolerated by the ruling class? How could the sacrifice of the martyrs be lived out when there was no longer anti-Christian hostility?

Hermits in the wilderness

It was in Egypt that Christians struggled towards an answer to this pressing question. The barren deserts provided an alternative martyrdom, a living death in the form of a life of extreme austerity in hostile surroundings. This was 'white martyrdom', the beginning of the monastic movement. Thousands fled to become hermits, seeking their individual salvation away from the churches and the cities. In so doing, some of them came into conflict with the organized Church.

The oldest Christian monastery in the world is situated in the Egyptian desert some forty miles from the Red Sea. Even driving there by car one wonders whether the monotonous sand, shimmering in the heat, will ever end. What it can have been like for fourth-century Christians, who walked or rode to get there, is impossible to imagine. There can have been nothing and nobody for mile, after mile, after mile. Even now there are only pipelines carrying oil from the rigs in the Red Sea. It was this emptiness, this desolation, that the desert fathers sought, and that was why St Antony chose to live in such an inhospitable place.

Born in about AD 251 in central Egypt, the son of a prosperous peasant farmer, he is reported to have decided on his solitary lifestyle when he heard the words of the Gospel, 'Go sell all that you have and give to the poor.' This was Jesus's advice to a rich young man who asked him how he could find eternal life. Antony took the words literally, sold up, and withdrew from his home village. He soon acquired such a reputation for asceticism that people poured out from Alexandria to visit him. He crossed the Nile to flee from his admirers and set up home in the desert near the Red Sea, the site of the present monastery. There he encountered an older hermit, called Paul, who became his adviser. At St Antony's there are mosaics depicting Paul and Antony meeting. Paul had a pet raven who brought him half a loaf every day. When Antony arrived the raven turned up with a whole loaf, and the pictures show the two hermits with their hands raised in blessing as the raven arrives with provisions.

Mosaic depicting St Antony dressed as a Coptic monk,
outside the monastery of St Antony in the Egyptian desert.

Antony's followers were not prepared to lose their spiritual director, so they pursued him into the desert. He helped them to establish the monastery and guided them in the ascetic life. Eventually he climbed the mountain which shelters the monastery and made his home in a cave. He had to climb down daily to fetch water and carry it up again, an exhausting task in the blazing heat. The well from which he drew water bubbles up almost miraculously within the monastery compound.

St Antony's is a gleaming white fortress surrounding a twin-towered church, which shelters a cluster of domes. Seen from the road it seems to have grown straight out of the sand. It is not like the well-ordered, disciplined monasteries of western Europe with their polished corridors, shadowy cloisters, beautiful plainsong services and silent, communal meals. In St Antony's, becoming a monk is still seen as a way of following in the steps of the martyrs. The monks wear a simple black cassock and a black bonnet, on which small golden crosses are embroidered. They seem much more individualistic than their Western counterparts. Discipline is not absent, but more relaxed, and each monk is expected to work out an appropriate level of fasting and prayer with his spiritual father. There is still something of the idiosyncrasy of the desert tradition in the life of the modern monk.

Father Dioscorus, a thin, smiling Egyptian monk with perfect English, explained that the essence of the monk's vocation was aloneness: 'Everyone here really wants to be a hermit.' Beyond the monastery were clusters of little round huts and stone buildings where those who had permission to do so lived in isolation. Even in the monastery, the monks eat their meals on their own. Each has a personal relationship with the abbot who acts as spiritual father.

What is the attraction of the desert? For Father Dioscorus it is the example of Antony. He feels that the ancient hermit is still very close to his present-day followers, and guides and inspires them.

St Antony was not a man who took thought for the future. He was probably illiterate and certainly did not see it as his role to write works which would perpetuate his memory or the memory of his life's achievements. But someone else did – his admirer St Athanasius, who was Bishop of Alexandria from AD 328 to 373. His biography of St Antony became a bestseller in both its original Greek and later in Latin. It spread to the West, where it had a profound impact on individuals who were drawn to the solitary life. Without it, the monastic life might never have started.

Much of what we know about the life of the monks comes from a fourth-century account of a journey through Egypt by a group of visitors from Jerusalem. They were impressed by the ability of the monks and hermits to put up with extreme hardship, and with the severe austerities that they practised. When such visitors came to the desert to learn from the monks they had to take care because, as they said, 'If one makes even a small error one can get lost in the desert and find one's life in danger.' One popular area for hermits was the area known as Scetis, in the western Nile Delta not far from Alexandria. It's a flat, sandy desert, full of salt deposits. Here men, and sometimes women, tended to live together in small communities. The visitors from Jerusalem reported, 'All the monks there have attained perfection. Indeed no one beset with imperfections could stay in that place, since it is rugged and inhospitable, lacking all the necessities of life.'

For all the difficulties, monasticism became almost a mass movement. Within about fifty years of St Antony's death there were reported to be seven hundred monasteries in the Palestinian and Egyptian deserts, as well as thousands of solitary hermits. No one can tell how many Christians sought refuge in the desert, though some scholars believe there may have been half a million of them. The scholar Sister Benedicta Ward, while warning against taking too literally the figures in the ancient texts, has written, 'It is no longer enough to dismiss such numbers at once as fantastic and imaginary; a lesson of caution has been learned from archaeological finds which have confirmed some of the claims which were once easily dismissed. It was, after all, a popular way of life.'

The desert fathers were regarded with great respect by many Christians. They were men who had found peace, loyal sons waiting for Christ as they would await the return of their father. All their wants were supplied by God. They were regarded as miracle workers, towers of spiritual strength on whose prayers others could rely. In their times it was not traffic fumes or other man-made gases which polluted the atmosphere, it was the devil and his demons.

OVERLEAF
The oldest monastery in the world,
founded by St Antony, in the desert
near the Red Sea.

The monks with their prayers were, as Sister Benedicta Ward has said, 'trees purifying the atmosphere by their presence'.

But not everyone looked on the desert fathers with approval. The authorities of the Roman Empire did not like men who not only avoided paying taxes, but also dodged conscription in the imperial army. They did not marry, so did not produce children, and this was considered anti-social. Sometimes their fiery passion for Christ led them into fanaticism, and even violence. Monks were stirred up to attacks on their pagan neighbours which included riots and the burning of temples.

The monks also got into trouble with the leaders of the Church. Living in the desert, seeking their own salvation, the desert fathers were not much concerned with matters ecclesiastical. In the life of St Antony there is no mention of communion, and elsewhere there are indications that many of the monks were not very regular communicants. They also seem to have had little respect for holy orders. The visitors from Jerusalem were asked by one of the great desert fathers, John of Lycopolis, whether any of them was ordained. There was a deacon present. He did not hold up his hand because he had heard that the ascetic would disapprove. But John somehow knew this and reprimanded him, not for being a deacon, but for telling a lie.

The desert fathers were reluctant teachers. They valued humility very highly and so were suspicious of any suggestion that they knew more than others, or had any particular wisdom to impart. John of Lycopolis asked his visitors from Jerusalem why they had taken so much trouble to visit 'poor, simple men who possess nothing worth seeing or admiring'. Indicating the monks' own reluctance to teach, John went on to say, 'We, from laziness, do not even wish to come out of our cave.' That attitude, of course, set the monks apart from a Church which did claim the authority to teach.

The monks also shunned the wisdom of books. Antony is reported to have said to a philosopher who questioned him, 'My book, O philosopher, is the nature of created things, and whenever I wish to read the words of God, it is in my hand.'

The monks believed that the way they tried to live their lives was based on the example of Jesus. He had gone into the desert to wrestle with the devil; so did they. Unlike the rich young man who turned away sadly from Jesus's challenge, they had sold all their possessions and lived as simply as possible. Jesus had not been one of those long-faced pious puritans who make life a misery for themselves and for everyone around them; nor were they. The visitors from Jerusalem described John of Lycopolis as having 'a bright and smiling face'; he and his fellow monks tried to practise Jesus's teaching that they should love one another. There are miraculous stories associated with the desert fathers. One visitor wrote, 'Why should we speak at length about their faith in Christ seeing that it can already move mountains? For many of them have stopped the flow of rivers and crossed the Nile dry-shod. They have slain wild beasts. They have performed cures, miracles, and acts of power, like those which the holy prophets and apostles worked. The saviour performs miracles through them in the same way.'

The desert fathers were sometimes so austere that their example seems irrelevant today. We dismiss as a crank the famous St Simon Stylites who lived on top of a pillar in the Syrian desert. In his time his critics accused him of spiritual vanity, but he won enormous support from local peasants and drew many recruits to the nearby monastery. He was considered so important to the Church's spiritual life that he was asked to agree to the deliberations of two important Church councils before their resolutions were finally accepted.

That was the Church's dilemma. It could not ignore the popularity of those like St Simon Stylites who sought their own Jesus, but yet it could not allow its own authority to be undermined by such ardent individualists. Basil, the Bishop of Caesarea, was well aware of that danger, and took steps to prevent the individualism of the desert taking hold of the monks in his charge. He rejected the ideal of solitude and believed that monks should live together in communities under a rule of obedience. He loathed spiritual ostentation and hysteria, and severely punished monks who fasted without permission. He also insisted that would-be monks underwent a period of training and made solemn vows. Basil's concern for moderation was important in later monasticism. He provided the framework for the rule of St Benedict, which became the norm for all monks of the Western Church from medieval times onward.

Desert fathers: the modern interpretation

The Egyptian monasteries of today stand in unbroken continuity with the past. Many of the monasteries house priceless manuscripts, icons and frescoes from the early days of the movement. Almost all the monks now belong to the Coptic, or Egyptian Orthodox Church. The Copts form a large minority in a Muslim country, comprising 10 per cent of the population. The young men who are recruited today are often well educated, with degrees in subjects such as chemistry, botany and engineering. The monks at St Antony's monastery hope in time to grow all their own food. Already they have olive and fruit trees in the monastery compound, but at the moment they are still dependent on a weekly van from Cairo which brings supplies. Recreation is often spent poring over seed catalogues. Father Dioscorus believes that it is the sheer silence of the desert which draws people to this way of life. Modern life is so full of pressure, noise and pollution that some will always be impelled to seek a simpler lifestyle.

The monks are evidence that from the third century there were individuals who believed that the most profound obedience to Jesus was to be found in a flight from normal society, and a search for a personal Jesus. Yet this could not have been a direct imitation of the life of Jesus. He was, as we have seen, a sociable person, not an ascetic. He was accused of being 'a glutton and a drunkard'. On the other hand, he did value poverty and simplicity. When he sent out his disciples to preach and heal he told them to take nothing for their journey. And then there is the story of the rich young man whom Jesus told to sell all his possessions and give the proceeds to the poor – the story which so inspired St Antony. But the most important link between Jesus and the hermits is in the story that Matthew, Mark and Luke tell of his own desert experience. They describe him – Mark briefly, Matthew and Luke in more detail – seeking a period of solitude after his baptism. Jesus went out to fight

St Simon Stylites, a famed hermit of the early Church,
sits on his column. Perhaps his passions are
not quite at peace, given the enormous size of
the serpent wound round the column. Or is it his
own pride at having sat there so long?
Silver reliquary, sixth century AD.

his battle with Satan alone. It was a time of temptation. Jesus encountered Satan in the Judaean wilderness. Here, suggested one of the Orthodox scholars whom I met, may lie a clue to the hidden Jesus.

I thought it would be appropriate to ask a scholar of the Eastern Church, which has always tried to preserve the spirituality of the hermits, why they were so attracted to the desert. I found that scholar in Oxford. Kallistos Ware, Bishop of Diokleia, was educated at an Anglican public school and at Oxford. After joining the Greek Orthodox Church he travelled widely in Greece and was particularly influenced by the time he spent at two famous monasteries, one on Mount Athos and one, at Patmos, where St John is said to have composed the book of Revelation. Here Kallistos Ware was ordained as a priest and took his vows as a monk. He returned to Oxford where he founded an Orthodox parish, and now lectures in Orthodox studies.

Wearing black robes beneath a flowing grey beard the bishop appeared to have shed all traces of his very English upbringing, but he still spoke with the accent bequeathed to him by Westminster School. He told me that the desert meant two things in Christian tradition, the one negative, the other positive. On the negative side it was seen as a land cursed by God because it did not have his blessings, particularly water without which we cannot live. Because it was cursed, it was regarded as a place where demons lurked. That was why the temptation of Jesus took place in the Judaean desert. He went out deliberately to face Satan. But at the same time the desert was also regarded as the place where you went to meet God. The children of Israel made their covenant with God in the wilderness of Sinai, and it was here that Moses received the ten commandments. The Old Testament prophets were lyrical about the wilderness, regarding it as the place where love bloomed between God and his people. They saw God as a jealous lover, who encountered his bride in the wilderness and lured her away. When Israel failed to be faithful, the prophet Jeremiah described God lamenting over her, 'I remember the devotion of your youth, your love as a bride, how you followed me in the wilderness . . . yet my people have forgotten me, days without number.'

Bishop Ware went on to explain how these two different traditions drew the fathers to the desert: 'We might think that a hermit who withdraws into the countryside is running away. But from the world-outlook of the early Christians, going out into the desert was not running away so much as confronting evil powers. So the hermits would be seen as the people in the front line, the Christian spiritual army fighting against the forces of evil, and in this way protecting the people in the cities. But the idea of the desert as the place where you can meet God continues. The hermit goes out to meet God.'

The bishop illustrated this from Athanasius's life of Antony. 'When Antony went into the deepest desert, where nobody had lived before, he heard demons shouting "Depart from what belongs to us, what are you doing here in the desert?" On the other hand Athanasius says that Antony loved the remote place where he settled.'

When I asked Bishop Ware whether the desire for a form of martyrdom was also important for the hermits, he replied 'I wouldn't want to try and explain the flight into the desert by that alone. But you have to remember that the early Christians lived under the Roman Empire and often faced persecution. In a sense they were already in an internal desert, cut off from society as a whole. When Christianity becomes official and is therefore adopted by society, then the more strict people felt the need to go out into the desert. That is part of the story, but the attraction of the desert is older than that.'

The bishop described the Egyptian monastic movement to me as 'not a rival to the Church, not anti-Church, but largely parallel, and not much inte-grated'. He believed there might well have been a schism or that the monks might even have been declared heretical if it had not been for Antony's biographer, Athanasius. As Bishop of Alexandria he had great influence in the Church and supported the hermits in his area. For him, Antony's way of life was the ideal, leading to a God-like state of perfection. The monks believed that by living austere lives and concentrating on prayer they would be transformed. Christ would live in them and through them; they would literally become immortal, 'all fire', as one ascetic put it. Athanasius himself taught that the aim of the spiritual life was divinization. As God became man in Jesus, so man would become God.

I then went to meet a Roman Catholic monk to ask him about the relationship between the desert fathers and the Church of their time. I thought it was important to talk to a Catholic because they regard their Church as being responsible for interpreting the scriptures and tradition. How do they deal with religious individualism? Father Luke Dysinger was on leave from his American Benedictine monastery, continuing his studies on the early Church at Oxford. We met at the presbytery in Reading where he was staying. When I arrived, Father Luke showed me into a dining room with light streaming through the windows and brightly painted walls, made more homely by the clatter of washing up from the kitchen next door. He was an impressive figure in his black Benedictine robes, tall and slim, with a fine but gentle face and a full head of prematurely grey hair.

Father Luke agreed that one of the strands in the monastic tradition was the sense that it was a continuation of something vital and idealistic which had existed before Constantine but was in danger of being lost when Christianity became respectable. He said to me, 'Whereas previously being a Christian meant you would not have access to any significant role in public life, suddenly that was all changed. To have any position of importance you had to be a Christian. The floodgates opened, the sense of zeal and a willingness to die for the faith faded into the background. So people looked back wistfully to that age of the martyrs. Monasticism was seen as a way of keeping martyr spirituality alive.'

'But then,' I suggested, 'that martyr spirituality must have found it difficult to accept the Church and its hierarchy who were by then very much part of society?'

Father Luke replied, cautiously, 'There were quite a few in the Egyptian monastic tradition who regarded the official structure of the Church, with its status and power, as problematic. You have little phrases that come from that period like, "Monks should avoid women and bishops" – women obviously, because they will entice you out of the monastery, but also bishops because they might ordain you. The fear was not so much that you'd be entering into the service of the Church, but that you'd be sacrificing all those means of deepening holiness which the monastic environment provided.'

So where, if not from the Church, did the men like St Antony get the Jesus who inspired them to live lives which involved such sacrifices? Father Luke pointed out that St Antony himself was first inspired by one of Jesus's sayings, and continued to draw his inspiration from the scriptures, reading them, pondering them and putting them into action. I found it fascinating that Father Luke, a Roman Catholic monk, felt that Christians today should go back directly to the words of Jesus rather than to the teaching of the Church. He said to me, 'St Antony's way of pondering the scriptures enabled him to become the primary symbol of a new way of living Christianity. This provided a challenge to institutional Christianity and a powerful force for reform as well. I think that can happen, and I think it needs to happen today.'

'He was with the wild beasts . . .' Christ cradles
the scorpion in his cupped hands during his
forty days in the wilderness. For the desert
fathers wild beasts were symbols of the passions.
To be at peace with them showed
spiritual maturity. From Stanley Spencer's
Christ in the Wilderness series, 1939.

Puzzles and riddles: forerunners of the Gospel

The spiritual insights of the early monks certainly provided a challenge to the institution of the Church. They are preserved in sayings and stories which read like a kind of folk wisdom, more intriguing than didactic. The utterances were often short, witty and enigmatic. The stories often have an exaggerated shaggy-dog flavour with an unexpected end. The point was not to teach any particular method or theology; it was to encourage real experience. The wisdom of the desert cannot be taught, but only caught. Their sayings do have parallels with the sayings of Jesus and may be a link with the hidden Jesus, because they have an unconventional flavour which is very close to some of Jesus's teaching. They are also put together very much as some scholars believe Jesus's sayings would have been, before they were edited and placed in the narrative of the Gospels.

The Gospels themselves retain strong indications that there was something anarchic in Jesus's teaching. I find this very attractive, although it is sometimes lost in over-familiarity. The camel going through the eye of a needle is a ridiculous idea, but it makes its point. There is the angry widow who becomes such a nuisance to a judge who is neglecting her case that she drives him into action just to get rid of her. And the rich fool who builds huge storehouses for his possessions only to be told he will die in the night. Jesus commends the crafty steward who wriggles out of his own bankruptcy by remitting the debts of others. Then there are his pithy sayings, which stimulate you to think without necessarily providing a prescription; 'You are the salt of the earth. . . .', 'Let what you say be simply "Yes" or "No". . . .', 'Judge not, that you be not judged. . . .', 'Do not be anxious for tomorrow, for tomorrow shall be anxious for itself.' Sometimes it looks as though these sayings have proved too much of a puzzle, and a layer of interpretation is added which makes their meaning more definite. The parable of the sower is a good example. Jesus talks about seed falling on four different kinds of soil, with different results. But Matthew, Mark and Luke report the disciples asking him for a more precise explanation; Jesus obliges, spelling out that the seed is the word of God and the different soils represent different reactions to the message of the Gospel. Most scholars believe that this layer of interpretation was added by the Church, and does not go back to Jesus. The anarchic, open-ended flavour of the original parable is lost; but the interpretation gives the clarity and definition that a struggling Church may have needed. So we have to peel back some of the layers of the biblical Gospels to find the Jesus of the sayings.

Since the nineteenth century scholars have tried to construct a theory of how the Gospels were composed. Most people now believe that Mark was written first, and John last, with Matthew and Luke coming in between. There is plenty of evidence that Matthew copied Mark, editing some bits out and expanding others. Luke probably used Mark too. One of the unsolved puzzles is that Matthew and Luke share rather a lot of material, which is not found in Mark. They must have got it from somewhere, but where?

Now it happens that most of this material is in the form of short sayings and parables. If you take it out from Matthew and Luke and string it together as one complete book it begins to resemble a collection like the sayings of the desert fathers. This material, embedded in the Gospels of Matthew and Luke, was called 'Q' by scholars. This stands for the German word *Quelle*, which means 'source'.

Some scholars are convinced that Q provides the earliest evidence for what Jesus was like. Fragments of his teaching – short, witty stories and riddles – were passed on by word of mouth and remembered. In a peasant society, where not many people could read or write, the spoken word was the most important form of communication. Wise sayings and stories were the best education that most people could get. It is probable that long before the narrative of the Gospels was composed, sayings of Jesus were in circulation among his followers. No doubt they added their own glosses and emphases along the way, like the interpretation of the parable of the seed. This theory makes it likely that Jesus was seen as a teacher of Wisdom, a peasant-sage. In the Old Testament Wisdom is sometimes personified as a figure who stands in the marketplace offering her wares free to the poor and simple. One of Jesus's best-loved sayings, probably because it is so beautifully set to music in Handel's *Messiah*, is, 'Come to me all who labour and are heavy-laden, and I will give you rest.' That invitation seems to some scholars to echo the call of Wisdom.

The possibility that Jesus was a wisdom teacher raises as many problems as it solves. What for instance would have been the Wisdom he taught? Wisdom is a very diverse concept. It can be simple and folksy like a popular riddle, or reasoned and sophisticated like the Wisdom of Solomon. Wisdom belongs to all religions. It was certainly found all over the Middle East in Jesus's time. There was Jewish Wisdom and Greek Wisdom and Egyptian Wisdom, and all had their part to play in the development of early Christianity. In the first few centuries there were many more sayings of Jesus in circulation than the ones now preserved in the four Gospels. There are even examples elsewhere in the New Testament. In the Acts of the Apostles St Paul says a moving farewell to the leaders of the Church in Ephesus. He ends, urging them to toil tirelessly on behalf of the weak, 'Remembering the words of the Lord Jesus, how he said, "It is more blessed to give than to receive." ' In fact, those precise words of Jesus are not recorded in any of the four biblical Gospels. So where did Paul get them from? There must have been alternative reports and memories of what Jesus said. Paul quoted this one, and we know that there were others because we have evidence that alternative texts were in circulation.

The Gospel of St Thomas

One of these sources was a Gospel ascribed to St Thomas, and one of the most exciting finds of recent years has been the discovery of a full text of this missing Gospel in a cave in Egypt. From it emerges a fascinating picture of Jesus, a spiritual Jesus which the Church has largely forgotten. It is easy to believe that Jesus uttered the saying quoted by St Paul, but what about this saying from the Gospel ascribed to St Thomas? 'Cleave the wood, and you will find me, lift the stone, and I am there.' Is it so easy to believe that the Jesus of the Church would have said that?

The site of the discovery, Nag Hammadi, is a fertile area on the banks of the Nile in Upper Egypt. It is a hot, humid region, full of sugar cane, wheat and barley fields, where the remains of a number of fourth-century monasteries have been discovered. In December 1945 a group of Egyptian farmers had tethered their camels by a high cliff to search for a natural fertilizer that could be found in the area. As they dug a man named Muhammad Ali accidentally unearthed a large sealed jar. At first he was reluctant to open it for fear that it contained a spirit which would object to being disturbed. But there had always been rumours that the area contained buried treasure from ancient times, and eventually Muhammad Ali decided to risk the wrath of the spirits in the hope of coming across gold.

According to Muhammad Ali's testimony gold did indeed fly up when he smashed the jar, but, disappointingly, it disappeared into thin air. What he saw were probably tiny fragments of papyrus which glistened like gold in the sunlight. Inside the jar he found thirteen papyrus books including the Gospel of St Thomas. Muhammad Ali thought he might have found valuable ancient manuscripts of biblical texts so he took the papyri to a nearby monastery, hoping that he might be able to sell them. The monks examined his find and quickly realized that they were not biblical writings, but ones which had been excluded from the New Testament. They sent Muhammad and his manuscripts away. Eventually the papyri came to the attention of scholars, who recognized their historical value.

The Gospel of Thomas has been a most important find. It was known to exist from earliest times, because some of the Church fathers refer to it. At the turn of the twentieth century some small and intriguing fragments of the Gospel, the earliest of which dates from around AD 200, had been discovered at Oxyrhynchus in Egypt. But these fragments were not enough to establish the sort of Gospel it was. Now we know it's a collection of what are claimed to be sayings of Jesus. Unlike other early Gospels it does not tell the story of Jesus's life, nor does it interpret the sayings. There is no birth of Jesus, no Crucifixion and no Resurrection. If Gospels reflect the concerns of early communities of Christians, it suggests powerfully that there were at least some communities who saw Jesus as a spiritual master rather than as a crucified and risen Lord.

The Gospel of Thomas claims that the secret to salvation lies, not in faith in the power of the sacrifice on the cross, but in understanding the sayings of Jesus, maintaining that anyone who discovers their interpretation will 'not taste death'. Some of the sayings in the other parchments found at Nag Hammadi actually go so far as to dismiss belief in the virgin birth and the bodily resurrection as naive misunderstandings.

The sayings attributed to Jesus in this Gospel include severe warnings against wealth and a comfortable life. They would have been appreciated by the desert fathers. But a more interesting parallel is that the sayings also emphasize the individual search for God, rather than the Church's authority over individuals. Jesus encourages his followers to be 'passers-by', observers rather than participants. The sayings do not have Jesus telling Christians what to do, but encouraging them to search for themselves. In the Gospel of Thomas, Jesus does not say that the kingdom of God is yet to come, but that it is present here and now and can be experienced by those who search for the meaning of the sayings. The Jesus of Thomas says, 'Whoever drinks from my mouth will become like me. I myself shall become that person, and the hidden things will be revealed to that person.' He seems to be saying that it is possible for us to become one with him, which is close to the teaching of the desert fathers.

There are parallels between the Gospel of St Thomas and of the New Testament. St John's Gospel does not describe a future kingdom, but promises eternal life which starts here and now. John also emphasizes the unity between Christ and his disciples: 'Abide in me, as I in you. . . . I am the vine, you are the branches.' St John's Gospel speaks of the need to be born anew, and promises those who are that they will see the kingdom of God. When the Pharisee Nicodemus asks how he, an old man, can be born again, Jesus says, 'Truly, truly we speak of what we know, and bear witness to what we have seen.' The synoptic Gospels, in which the role of Jesus as the way to God is far less clearly defined than in St John's Gospel, contain traces of similar sayings. In St Matthew's Gospel Jesus says that God 'Has hidden these things from the wise and understanding and revealed them to babes'. In St Mark's Gospel Jesus tells the disciples that they are privileged because to them is given 'the mystery of the kingdom of God', while to others 'all is in parables'. These are all indications that, to some at least, the teaching of Jesus came with special knowledge which was available only to those who search and understand.

Another piece of evidence that Jesus might have been a teacher of a hidden, elusive sort of wisdom comes from a movement in the early days of the Church whose followers saw salvation in terms of knowledge. They were called Gnostics from the Greek word *gnosis*, which means knowledge. We usually use the word 'knowledge' to mean information, head knowledge, but *gnosis* actually means inner, psychological experience. The content of *gnosis* is the secret of human origins and destiny and the route to redemption. Gnostics distinguished between the true God and a lesser God who created the world. They saw Jesus as a semi-divine figure, not a real human being. He was a revealer of cosmic mysteries rather than a redeemer. They thought that they were an élite, possessing spiritual knowledge, while other Christians were bogged down in dogma handed down to them second-hand. *The Gospel of Truth*, one of the writings discovered at Nag Hammadi, says, 'He who thus is going to have knowledge knows when he came and whither he is going.'

An Egyptian bishop described *gnosis* as the knowledge of 'Who we were and what we have become, where we were, where we were placed, whither we hasten, from what we are redeemed, what birth is and what rebirth.' Unlike the desert fathers, the Gnostics came to be regarded as heretics by the Church. The bishops were particularly concerned that the Gnostics' Jesus was too personal – a figure who related so much to individual dreams and hopes that he might not inspire the fervour necessary to create martyrs, and martyrs were essential if Christianity was not to succumb to the persecutions of the early centuries. The bishops also realized that there could be no authoritative Church if individuals were to have freedom to interpret the sayings of Jesus in purely psychological terms.

There are scholars who argue that the four Gospels of which the Church approved were selected, at least in part, because they supported the Apostles' claim to authority – an authority the bishops maintained they had inherited. Matthew, Mark and Luke all describe Peter's moment of insight when he suddenly grasps that Jesus was 'the Christ'. Matthew expands the incident, and has Jesus giving Peter a unique authority, 'the keys of the kingdom'. Peter is 'the rock' on which the Church is to be built. The moment of recognition is followed by the Transfiguration, in which Jesus appears in his heavenly glory to the inner circle of disciples, Peter, James and John. The giving of authority is confirmed by some kind of vision or revelation. In John's Gospel it is after the Resurrection that Peter is given authority in an appearance by the Sea of Galilee. The authority to forgive or retain sins is also given, according to John, when the risen Jesus meets with his disciples in the upper room and breathes on them to give them the Holy Spirit. In St Matthew's Gospel the risen Jesus tells the eleven: 'All authority in heaven and on earth has been given to me. Go therefore and make disciples of all nations, baptizing them in the name of the Father and of the Son and of the Holy Spirit, teaching them to observe all that I have commanded you; and, lo, I am with you always to the close of the age.' The New Testament Gospels do seem to show that Jesus handed his authority to the Apostles, and in particular to Peter, and so only they could have handed on that authority. In this way, according to the Roman Catholic, Orthodox and Anglican Churches, the Apostolic Succession was established, making the Bishops today the successors of the Apostles.

A Gospel which does not mention the Resurrection or the Transfiguration

The Transfiguration of Christ is an important theme in Eastern Orthodoxy because it reveals Jesus's divine nature and identity. The Old Testament prophets Moses and Elijah are shown on either side of Christ, with the Apostles Peter, John and James transfixed with awe at his feet. Mosaic of the sixth century in the monastery of St Catherine in the Sinai Desert in Egypt.

would have been anathema to those who wanted to trace the Church's authority back to Jesus. The American scholar Elaine Pagels, who translated a number of the Nag Hammadi manuscripts, points out that the orthodox position was only reached by repressing alternatives. For example, the Gospels describe Mary Magdalene as the first to witness the Resurrection. In Mark's version she arrives at the tomb, with some of the other women who have supported Jesus, 'very early on the first day of the week'. In Luke's Gospel she returns to tell the other disciples that the Lord has risen, but they do not believe her. In spite of her position in the narrative, the later Church traces authority through Peter and not through Mary. Some of the Nag Hammadi texts show disputes and jealousies between Peter and Mary, suggesting that there really was a power struggle in early Christianity, which was won by the more authoritarian party. Mary Magdalene's story was downgraded, Peter's was elevated.

Near to the site where the manuscripts were discovered are the remains of an ancient monastery. Could the Nag Hammadi texts have been buried by an unorthodox monk who was afraid that the ecclesiastical authorities would have destroyed them? We now know that there were many copies of St Thomas's Gospel and that it was particularly popular in Egypt. Did the Church destroy as many copies as it could because the Gospel challenged its authority?

What has become increasingly clear, not least through the discovery of the Nag Hammadi manuscripts, is that early Christianity was extremely varied. There were Christians who believed in a Jesus very different from the Jesus of later orthodoxy, who accepted Gnostic interpretations alongside, and perhaps in preference to, the four Gospels. These Christians believed that their personal knowledge of Jesus was more direct and authentic than the teaching of bishops, backed up by the claim to inherit the authority given to the Apostles. Some of them were so convinced Jesus spoke to them individually that they came to reject the bishops, who then, as now, tried to persuade Church members that they had to believe what they were told.

As Jesus was a historical figure it is important to discover what historical weight we should put on St Thomas's Gospel. Is its picture of Jesus as the giver of secret sayings an authentic portrait? In one sense it obviously is, in that from the early days of the Church it was popular with Christians, which means that those living near to the time of Jesus regarded it as a satisfactory picture of him.

And then of course, there is Q. If the sayings common to Matthew and Luke are the edited version of an earlier sayings source, then we have a second sayings Gospel hidden in the heart of the New Testament, like a subversive time bomb ticking away. Q has no birth narrative or Resurrection. Its portrait of Jesus is very much that of a teacher of wisdom. If you compare Q to Thomas, it is clear that there are many sayings which are similar to each other. Thomas has its own version of the parable of the seed, which some scholars think is in an even more primitive form than the version found in Mark or Q. If this is true, then some of the sayings of Jesus in the Gospel of Thomas may be among the most authentic that we have.

If Thomas was the preferred Gospel for a large number of Christians, they must have found in it a recognizable and attractive picture of Jesus. In his book on the Gospel of Thomas the American scholar Marvin Meyer writes, 'The readers of the Gospel of Thomas are invited to join the quest for the meaning of life by interpreting the cryptic and enigmatic "hidden sayings" of Jesus. . . . The quest is to be undertaken with commitment, and while the way taken may be upsetting, people will attain insight and rest if only they persevere.' Meyer goes on to point out that the sayings of Jesus might not just be upsetting for individuals, they might also upset society. They suggest that families should be rejected, that followers of Jesus should be 'passers-by' and therefore not obsessed with the normal activities of life, not sharing the usual ambitions. The luxurious lifestyle of the rich is ridiculed and those involved in business are excluded from God's kingdom. Traditional religion is also undermined by sayings which pour scorn on priestly piety. The sayings of Jesus in the Gospel of Thomas do not seem to offer a dogmatic moral code, a list of 'don'ts'. The point is that the listener or reader has to complete the riddle for him or herself; the meaning of the saying can only be created by the hearer's experience. In this sense Thomas has links to Q, to the Gnostics and to the desert fathers.

The Greek Cynics: parallels with Jesus

There is another link in this search for the hidden Jesus which leads in quite a different direction. In the town of Bolton in the North of England lives an Anglican parish priest, the Reverend Gerald Downing, who somehow manages to find time despite running an active church to continue his studies

An early Christian sarcophagus decorated with pagan and Christian
motifs, including a Good Shepherd and a seated philosopher.
Jesus's teachings on simplicity of life and the importance
of learning from nature echo those of the Greek
Cynic philosophers who traced their beliefs back to
a fourth-century sage, Diogenes. From the church
of St Saveur, Brignoles, France.

on the sayings of Jesus, and to argue his case that much of the teaching is based on what at first sight appears to be a highly unlikely source, the Greek Cynics. The Cynic school of philosophy was founded in the fourth century BC, by Diogenes who came from Sinope on the Black Sea but spent most of his life in Corinth. His followers became wandering teachers, notable for the simplicity of their lifestyle and easily recognizable by their shabby clothing. Cynics always wore a simple cloak and carried a stick and usually a bag for their food, but no change of clothes. There are obvious similarities between the Cynics' baggage, or lack of baggage, when they set out on the road, and the instructions that Jesus gave his disciples when he sent them forth: 'He charged them to take nothing for their journey except a staff; no bread, no bag, no money in their belts.' The Cynics, who saw their role in life as teachers, stressed freedom as man's true destination. Freedom meant not becoming involved in the pursuit of wealth, office, fame or any of the other objectives to which most of us dedicate our lives. When achieved, the Cynics said, these aims do not satisfy but become burdens.

As I listened to Gerald Downing expound his theory I found myself thinking how relevant Cynic philosophy is to life today. We can see how those who gain riches never seem to have enough. They worry about catching up with others who have even more money. Those in high office or important jobs spend their time worrying about keeping them. Those who achieve fame find themselves caught in a continuous battle to preserve a degree of privacy while at the same time keeping themselves in the limelight.

The Cynics taught friendship, not competition with each other. They also subverted authority, teaching that Cynics should neither be masters nor accept others as masters. There should be no domination, because God was the only master. Downing told me about the Cynic philosopher Epictetus who was once threatened by someone who said, 'I'll show you I'm your master.' 'Oh?' he replied. 'How can you be? Zeus has set me free. Do you really think he's going to allow a son of his to be enslaved?' Downing explained how Jesus's lifestyle was similar to that of a Cynic teacher: 'He's simply teaching by his own example. So far as we can trust the records, he lives simply, he relates to people, he does without a secure home base, he travels light and encourages his followers to do so.'

There are obvious parallels, too, between the teaching of Jesus and the teaching of the Cynics. Jesus said, 'Therefore do not be anxious about tomorrow, for tomorrow will be anxious for itself.' He also advised his followers to think of the birds of the air who neither sowed nor reaped, and – more importantly still from a Cynic point of view – did not store up in barns. Gerald Downing said to me, 'Jesus is like the Cynics in that he takes the same example from the animal world as the Cynics. He takes the example of birds which do not store anything.'

I wondered whether Jewish, as opposed to Greek, literature contained examples of people being advised to imitate animals. Downing replied, 'Yes, but there is a fundamental difference. In the book of Proverbs the ant was chosen as an example of virtue. The ant is a creature which works hard to store up things – completely the opposite of the bird.' In other words, the Jewish wisdom tradition was more about hard work and discipline than about the freedom of birds. In that example, Jesus seems closer to the Cynics than to the Jewish tradition. Jesus also echoes the Cynics in the way he subverted authority. He said, 'You are not to be called rabbi, for you have one teacher, and you are all brethren. And call no man your Father on earth for you have one father, who is in heaven.' It always strikes me as strange that, in spite of that verse from St Matthew, Christian priests should be called 'Father'. Cynics, and I am sure Jesus too, would have found it even stranger if they had heard a bishop being addressed as 'My Lord'. The Cynics were insistent that they should not be regarded as superior because they taught.

There is one difficulty with Gerald Downing's theory. The Cynics were Greek philosophers. Jesus was a Jew, and the examples in his teaching, even the reference to the birds, are all taken from rural Jewish life. Downing agreed that the only literature which was referred to in the Gospel tradition was Jewish, but he went on to say, 'When you look at the actual content, when you look at the themes that are majored on, when you look at the kind of attitudes which are expressed and lived, then you'll find yourself very much closer to pagan Cynicism than to anything we find in our Jewish sources. The only way it makes sense to me is to think that the culture of Jesus's society had already been infiltrated to some extent by Cynic views. The views most likely came from Gadara in Syria, not very far south of Galilee. I think one thing which has emerged from recent archaeological excavations there is that it was the Athens of Syria.' If Gerald Downing is right, Cynic preachers might have been a familiar sight to Jesus. Mark and Matthew describe Jesus healing in what may have been the area of Gadara. Matthew's Gospel also says that crowds came out from Decapolis, the 'ten towns' of which Gadara was one, to hear Jesus preach.

Gerald Downing's theory has not met with universal scholarly approval, because there is no direct evidence that Cynics were active in Syria or Galilee at the time of Jesus. But it remains a tantalizing possibility. What struck me most about Gerald was his patent sincerity. He was a scholar who really did imitate his Cynic Jesus in his own life. With long, straggly hair, a bushy Victorian beard and an ill-fitting coat, he clearly took no care for appearances. He did not hold the kind of office considered desirable by most academics, such as a university professorship, but he bore no resentment about that; he was content to be a simple parish priest. Bolton has always regarded itself as a down-to-earth working town and has no illusions of glamour, and Gerald Downing's parish on the outskirts could certainly not be regarded as glamorous. He was starkly honest about himself, saying, 'Although I am the author of books about Jesus and Cynicism, I have to accept a fair degree of hypocrisy. I claim a commitment to this human and divine Jesus, and I suppose my wife and I do live fairly simply, but none the less with a vast amount more wealth around us than Jesus, or the pagan followers of similar philosophies.' Seeing the small, modern house in which he lived, and its simple furnishings, I said, 'Come on, you do much more than most to live like a Cynic.'

He replied, 'Well, I do try to suggest that there are possibilities of pushing one's life a little nearer to the rigorous lifestyle Jesus adopted. In my own life I'm trying to do it, but I'm a long way from just one cloak, a satchel and a staff. Keeping a second-hand car for seven years instead of exchanging it is a minor gesture.'

Whether or not Jesus was directly influenced by Cynic preachers, we do have evidence which suggests that the desert fathers were often compared to Cynics by their contemporaries. The rough and ready lifestyle of the monks and their anarchic wisdom were comprehensible, if sometimes irritating, to their pagan neighbours because they were not the only people pursuing an alternative lifestyle. Cynics would have been as familiar a sight on the streets of Alexandria as they were in any other of the cities of the Roman world.

If I am honest, I have to confess that I have the same difficulty with Gerald Downing's Jesus as I had with Jesus the rebel. He did not seem to me a sufficiently unusual person to have inspired his followers to found the Church. Could the figure behind two thousand years of Christianity really have been nothing more than an oddball teacher wandering around the countryside in a remote part of the Roman Empire? Gerald Downing himself did not think that Cynicism explains everything about Jesus. He disagreed with those scholars who believe their interpretations of Jesus tell the whole story, saying to me, 'I don't believe that Jesus was a wisdom teacher and nothing more. I accept that there were very traditional Jewish strands which would have been part of Jesus's life, and had no influence from the Cynics. I share the faith of later Christians who came to believe that God in some way shared the life of Jesus, that there was more to him than either a prophet or Cynic.'

A Jesus for today

What I took away from my conversation with Gerald Downing was that it is perfectly possible to believe that Jesus was unique in his relationship to God, but that at the same time he taught that the way to respond to God is to be free from possessions and ambition – just as the Jesus of the Gospel of Thomas taught, and just as the desert fathers lived. That makes this Jesus particularly relevant to the end of the millennium. Scholars of all schools accept that two thousand years ago Jesus stood out against the society of his day, either as an apocalyptic prophet or a social revolutionary, or as the Jesus of wisdom, and was so threatening to authority that even the Church buried some of the evidence about him. What I like about Jesus the Cynic is that he stands out against the consumerism of our day. He exposes what I believe to be the great heresy of today, that economic growth will solve the world's problems. In India, Africa and large parts of Central and South America the amazing global economic growth of the last fifty years has not even solved the most obvious problem it ought to answer, poverty. Nor has it solved the problems of the so-called richer world. It has certainly not produced the freedom which the Cynics taught us we could all enjoy. Those of us who have prospered from the new wealth are still enslaved to property. We are taught to believe that we can never be free, never have enough, because if we ever become content with what we have, who will buy the ever-increasing goods and services we have to create to ensure the continuation of economic growth? Here I must utter just one word of caution. Jesus the teacher of wisdom has sometimes been accused of applauding poverty. One of the great Christians of our century, Mother Teresa of Calcutta, has faced the same charge. Neither, I think, want to see destitution, but they do not want us to worship wealth. It says something about the spiritual blindness of our time that their attack on the selfish accumulation of riches should be misinterpreted as a glorification of poverty.

The Cynic teachers were individuals and had no organization to support them. No one gave them rules or passed judgement on the orthodoxy of their teaching. As the millennium approaches, more and more Christians seem to be seeking their individual way to God. Like the desert fathers, they find the Church is obsessed with itself: women priests, what to do about falling congregations, Christian unity, sexual morality and many other issues which, no matter how rigorous the arguments on either side, are in essence issues of organization. When the Church does speak, it seems to address society as a whole rather than the individual. It speaks out on the problem of poverty in wealthy societies, on marriage and the family, and on the environment. But the Church does not provide wisdom for the individual, it does not cater for the individual's hunger for spirituality. That hunger will inevitably be shown in visions and prophecies at a time like the millennium, when people look to the future, especially since many see a dark age ahead. The leading Roman Catholic archbishop in Ireland has warned that such visions and prophecies should be treated with great caution. But he cannot ignore the old saying, 'Where there is no vision, the people perish.' The Church itself needs to recover the voice of the prophet and the voice of the wisdom teacher. It cannot remain just the judge.

Humanity seems to have lost its way. Even science has lost its certainty, and the fashionable philosophy of post-modernism says there can be no certainty. Materialism has failed. Although there is more of everything, no one is satisfied. The pace of change gets faster and faster. Old customs collapse but are not replaced by new social constraints. Institutions which one inspired loyalty no longer command respect. Even the family is under threat. We know the price of everything but the value of nothing. We make discoveries, manipulate genes, invent machines which think for us; but we seem to lack the moral vision to consider whether discoveries and inventions are beneficial or harmful. We use them regardless of the consequences. We are being swept along by a tide of technology. Will we be dashed against the rocks, or will we reach calmer waters?

When the Church was first threatened by worldliness Christians fled to the desert to keep what they believed was the true flame burning. In the dark ages which followed the collapse of the Roman Empire, which had played such a role in the spread of Christianity, it was the self-contained monasteries which kept the flame alight – not only the flame of faith, but the flame of learning and wisdom. Now once again, it seems, Christians are finding ways of fleeing from society. Some withdraw by belonging to house churches, others by going on retreat. Monasteries and convents still provide sanctuary.

Retreat from the pagan West

My travels in Egypt ended with a visit to St Catherine's monastery in the Sinai desert, which nestles in a valley surrounded by great red mountains. Its buildings date from the sixth century. The rounded tip of the tower of the ancient church can just be seen above the high wall. Within the walls there is a mosque, which was built, I was told, to discourage Muslims from attacking the monastery. The Bedouins, the desert people, who helped to build the monastery, were originally Christian but later converted to Islam. In the church there is a magnificent mosaic of the Transfiguration, glittering even in the semi-darkness. It was there that I met a young Englishman who had been admitted as a monk; until recently, only Greeks were allowed to join.

Father Nilus was a large, stout man who retained the West Country accent of his native Crediton. Long black curls and a beard surrounded a pale face that bore a shy but determined expression. As a student he had decided that the Church of England did not satisfy his spiritual needs, and he had joined the Greek Orthodox Church. He had fled from what he regarded as his pagan homeland to the remote desert monastery. When I met him he had just returned from his first trip back to England, where he had been sent on a course to learn about the restoration of ancient manuscripts. He confessed to me, 'I ate nothing but fish and chips for the first week.'

I asked, 'So how are you coping without them? Any withdrawal symptoms?'

The black-robed monk laughed. 'No, I'm only too happy to be back here. I found Britain more pagan than ever.' He was glad to have returned to a life of prayer. The first liturgy of his day started at four in the morning and could last until eight o'clock. What, I wondered, could so much worship achieve? Father Nilus explained, 'The desert fathers struggled against the darkness of

OVERLEAF
The Greek Orthodox monastery of St Catherine lies at
the foot of Mount Sinai. It is a treasure house
of icons and ancient manuscripts. It also encloses
the 'burning bush', associated with Moses, which is
sacred to Jews, Moslems and Christians.

their times, and we are struggling to keep that tradition alive. Through our prayers we are struggling against the darkness of modern paganism.'

St Catherine's monastery can now be approached by road and is open to tourists for a few hours on most days. I met a party of Australian pilgrims led by their parish priest, who was a member of a Roman Catholic religious order. Their pilgrimage had been organized by a young woman called Emma Loveredge who, like Father Nilus, came from England. She had first come to the Sinai desert to study the icons of St Catherine's monastery for her PhD in early Christian art. There she found pilgrims who were, as she put it, 'sick and miserable' from the heat and unfamiliar food, and so she had decided to set up an organization which would provide better support for them in coping with the extremities of the place. This had grown into a travel company, Wind, Sand and Stars, specializing in the Sinai desert. Emma still retained her particular interest in pilgrims. This small, thin Englishwoman, with her brown hair hidden under a *kafia*, the embroidered cotton head-dress that the Bedouin wear, had also established a special relationship with the people of the desert. Many of them still live their traditional life in tents, travelling by camel between the winter and summer pastures of their goats and sheep. They appear formidably hardy to strangers, but Emma Loveredge has found them 'very attractive, friendly and happy, with a very high standard of dealing with other people'.

When I asked Emma what attracted pilgrims and other tourists to the desert she said, 'They seem to want to discover who they are for themselves. Even those with a culture of their own seem to feel a lack of spiritual life in Western countries. I think that's because there is no way they can find it. There is a lack of holy people who are also teachers.'

The pilgrims are also fleeing materialism. Emma Loveredge often sends them into the desert with no baggage except their toothbrushes. She told me, 'When they are here in Sinai, they just want to sit in the desert.' In a booklet that she has written for those who travel with her she has summarized the tradition followed by the desert fathers as simplicity of life, waiting for God and a struggle against darkness. That would also seem to summarize the life which those pilgrims of hers who just want to sit in the wilderness are searching for.

To me, the struggle between the individual searching for God and the institution which fears that all will be lost if rules are not laid down was symbolized by the great mountain rising out of the red rocks of the desert, Mount Sinai. I rode most of the way up the mountain on a camel, uncomfortably wedged between two pegs on the front and back of the saddle, but anything was better than walking in the intense midday heat. Even the camels could not manage the final ascent, and so for more than half an hour I had to scramble up rough steps hewn out of the mountain. It was worth all the effort to reach the summit and look out across the desert where, according to the Bible, the Israelites had wandered for forty years. I was struck as never before by the sheer audacity of Moses, who had led his people into that inhospitable place where water was so rarely seen and it seemed no crops could grow. They may have been slaves in Egypt, but they had been softened by the conveniences of what was a highly civilized society. Like Father Nilus who missed his British fish and chips, the Israelites longed for 'the fish we ate in Egypt . . . the cucumbers, the melons, the leeks, the onions, and the garlic. . . .' Moses had earlier experience of the desert so he knew the problems he would face, but he was confident that the Lord would provide. According to the Book of Exodus, God did provide, just at the point when the children of Israel were on the verge of a mutiny, complaining that they had been brought from the fleshpots of Egypt to die of hunger. God sent miraculous quails for them to eat, and 'manna' from heaven, which was a kind of bread. When the children of Israel feared they would die of thirst, God told Moses to strike the rock of Mount Horeb and water flowed.

Here on the top of Mount Sinai Moses received the commandments, the laws which bound the people of Israel to their God. He is portrayed as the great law-giver, the founder of Judaism. Down below in the desert the hermits and monks of early Christianity rejected the conventions of the Church of their day to seek their individual salvation. The English monk Father Nilus has followed in their footsteps, turning from the Church in which he was brought up to seek something beyond it. Emma's pilgrims were still seeking their own answers.

During the perilous descent, which we made on foot, we passed the gateway where a priest used to hear the confessions of penitent pilgrims

OVERLEAF
Mark Tully on the summit of Mount Sinai.

before they ascended the holy mountain. Here I asked Emma whether I was right to think of her pilgrims as searching for themselves. She replied, 'Some, particularly the younger ones, are searching for their own individuality. I'm not so sure about the older ones. They want to stay within their own Churches, but they are looking for something more than those institutions have given them.'

A new role for the Church

So what can the Church do about such aspirations? Its tradition has been to insist that it has a monopoly of wisdom, and it has always been deeply suspicious of inspired individuals. Perhaps it is also deeply suspicious of the anarchic, witty Jesus who can still be found in the biblical Gospels. Think of the story of the Pharisee and the publican, in which Jesus mocks the self-regard of the conventionally religious. Or his scathing attack on those who 'load men with burdens hard to bear' while 'you yourselves do not touch the burdens with one of your fingers'. So often the Church has ironed out all the criticism of authority, all the humour, all the exaggeration and teasing sharpness of Jesus's teaching. In a sense it is the Church that has driven Jesus into hiding.

But it is this Jesus who is in demand now. People long for a divine figure who is also human, who is, like Jesus in the Gospel of Thomas, a twin brother to the soul. He is always on the edge of things, a passer-by, who still stands in the marketplace, like the figure of Wisdom, calling out to the distracted crowds, 'Come to me, all you that labour and I will give you rest.' He has never been a figure with whom the Church has found it easy to live, but if the Church is not able to recover the wise Jesus from its history it will no longer be able to provide the shade that prevents the lamp of faith from being blown out. We will then either have no Christianity, or an extreme, fundamentalist, even violent form of that faith. I believe it will be very important for the Church to rediscover the hidden Jesus in the third millennium.

Afterword

Studying *Lives of Jesus* for two years has brought me face to face with history. India, where I have lived for many years, is a land of myths, and I had begun to think that the Jesus of history did not matter any more than the Krishna of history. All that mattered was the Jesus of faith, the Jesus in whom people believed. I was even in danger of forgetting that Jesus did live, that there was independent, non-Christian historical evidence to prove that there was a first-century Jew called Jesus who was crucified, and whose followers continued to believe in him after his death.

The history of Jesus has also reminded me that, during his life, he was a very minor figure. If he was a social rebel, his rebellion failed. If he was a Jewish prophet of the end to come, that end did not come. If he was a miracle worker, there were plenty of others around at the time. He may have been a well-above-average teacher of wisdom, or a more attractive preacher than most, but that does not make him particularly unusual in the context of later history. What I have now concluded is that the miracle of Jesus is the Church which emerged from such humble beginnings in such a remote part of the Roman Empire. If Jesus had not been unique, surely he would have disappeared from the pages of history when he was crucified – he would have been just another man who fell foul of the Roman Empire. The Roman historian Tacitus would not have mentioned Jesus if his followers had not been still causing trouble.

But I also now have a problem with history. Jesus the Pharisee, or the prophet, or the revolutionary, or the teacher of hidden wisdom, is not a sufficiently remarkable figure to explain the Church. I would agree with those scholars I have met who say that without the Resurrection there would have been no Church. Here I return to myth. It does not seem to me any longer a question of knowing precisely what happened after Jesus died. We cannot know whether he really appeared in some physical form to the disciples, although I now certainly believe that the founders of the Church were convinced he did. What matters is the power of the myth of the Resurrection, which inspired at least some of the earliest Christians to believe that God so loved us that he gave his Only-Begotten Son for us. So for me, at least, the Jesus of history, the comparatively insignificant Jew, proves that there was some event or events after his death which created the myth that he was divine.

Unfortunately the word 'myth' has been so debased that many people now think it means untruth. We have been beguiled by our successes in science into believing that only what we have been taught to regard as facts matter. We forget the limitations of our factual knowledge. We forget that poetry, legend and myth have always been necessary to express what matters to us most deeply. After meeting historians who offer different interpretations of the facts we know about Jesus, I believe the history of the Church shows that, whatever happened after Jesus died, the Resurrection was a sufficiently powerful event to inspire an answer to the universal mysteries of suffering and death. It is an answer which has proved meaningful to many ever since. I at least have never found an answer to those mysteries in science, or indeed history.

Chronology

Further Reading

Jesus the God

BURRIDGE, Richard A., *Four Gospels, One Jesus*, SPCK, 1994

FUNK, Robert, and HOOVER, Roy, and the Jesus Seminar, *The Five Gospels*, Simon & Schuster, 1995

GRIFFITHS, Bede, *The Marriage of East and West*, HarperCollins, 1982

WRIGHT, Tom, *Who Was Jesus?*, SPCK, 1992

Jesus the Jew

MURPHY-O'CONNOR, Jerome, *The Holy Land*, Oxford University Press, 1986

SANDERS, Ed, *The Historical Figure of Jesus*, Penguin, 1995

VERMES, Geza, *Jesus the Jew*, SCM Press, 1973; 4th edition, 1992

Jesus the Rebel

CROSSAN, Dominic, *The Historical Jesus: The Life of a Mediterranean Jewish Peasant*, HarperCollins, 1991

CROSSAN, Dominic, *The Essential Jesus*, HarperCollins, 1996

HORSLEY, Richard A., *Jesus and the Spiral of Violence: Popular Jewish Resistance in Roman Palestine*, Fortress Press, 1993

The Hidden Jesus

DOWNING, Gerald F., *Cynics and Christian Origins*, T. & T. Clarke, 1992

MEYER, Marvin, ed., *The Gospel of Thomas: The Hidden Sayings of Jesus*, HarperCollins, 1993

PAGELS, Elaine, *The Gnostic Gospels*, Penguin, 1990

WARD, Benedicta, *The Lives of the Desert Fathers*, translated by Norman Russell, Cistercian Publications, 1981

General

BORG, Marcus, *Meeting Jesus Again for the First Time*, HarperCollins, 1994

CHADWICK, Henry, *The Early Church*, Penguin, 1993

Credits

BBC BOOKS would like to thank the following for providing photographs and for permission to reproduce copyright material. While every effort has been made to trace and acknowledge all copyright holders, we would like to apologize should there have been any errors or omissions.

Page 8 © BBC/photo: Bill Robinson; P.13 © John Miller/Collections; P.20 The Board of Trinity College, Dublin; P.25 Museo di Capodimonte, Naples/SCALA; P.33 The Ancient Art and Architecture Collection Ltd; P.36 © Rajinder KR/Images of India Picture Agency; P.37 Museo di San Marco, Florence/Bridgeman Art Library; P.40–1 © Christophe Boisvieux/Frank Spooner Pictures; P.48 © Yoga Savith; P.51 photo © Eileen Tweedy; P.61 Benaki Museum, Athens/SCALA; P.66–7 © Fred Mayer/ Magnum Photos Ltd; P.74–5 Robert Harding; P.79 National Gallery, London/ Bridgeman Art Library; P.86 photo Andy Farrington © BBC; P.94–5 © Tower of David Museum of the History of Jerusalem/photo Yoram Leheman; P.98–9 Arch of Titus, Rome/SCALA; P.106–7 and 110–11 © Fred Mayer/Magnum Photos Ltd; P.118–19 © Penny Tweedie/ Colorific!; P.122–3 Robert Harding; P.138 Victoria & Albert Museum/Bridgeman Art Library; P.142–3 © Fred Mayer/Magnum Photos Ltd; P.150–1 Catacomb of Priscilla, Rome/SCALA; P.155 © Marlborough Gallery, New York/Art Resource, New York; P.158–9 Stanza di Raffaelo, Vatican/SCALA; P.161 Hagia Sofia, Istanbul/SCALA; P.164–5 San Vitale, Ravenna/SCALA; P.177 and 180–1 © Angela Tilby; P. 184 © C. M. Dixon; P.189 Art Gallery of Western Australia/ Bridgeman Art Gallery, © Estate of Stanley Spencer All Rights Reserved DACS; P.196–7 © E. Tzaferis S.A.; P.200–1 © John Parker/By kind permission of Monsieur Jean Martin, Président des Amis du Vieux Brignoles, Musée du Pays Brignolais, Provence; P.208–9 © A. M. Hyncica/Wind, Sand & Stars, London; P.212–13 © Angela Tilby.

THE QUOTATION ON PAGE 34 comes from *Sources of Indian Tradition*, Vol. I, by Ainslie T. Embree. Copyright © 1988 by Columbia University Press. Reprinted with permission of the publisher.

Travel

WIND, SAND & STARS are specialist travel operators in the Sinai desert and can be contacted at 2 Arkwright Road, London NW3 6AD

Index

Numbers in *italics* refer to pages with illustrations.